A Country Compendium

A Country Compendium

GODFREY BASELEY

Text Illustrations by
Alex Jardine

SIDGWICK & JACKSON
LONDON

First published in Great Britain in 1977
by Sidgwick and Jackson Limited

0283982225

Copyright © 1977 Godfrey Baseley

Jacket illustrations by Jan Mitchener

ISBN 0 283 98222 5

Made and printed in Great Britain by
The Garden City Press Limited
Letchworth, Hertfordshire SG6 1JS
for Sidgwick and Jackson Limited
1 Tavistock Chambers, Bloomsbury Way
London WC1A 2SG

Contents

PART SIX

Flowers and Trees

Foreword

My filing tray was full to overflowing. Not one more flimsy would it hold without spilling over on to the floor. There was at least a six-month accumulation. It was no good, everything would have to stop while I put the system in order.

It was not quite as simple as that because when I pulled out the first of the drawers I found a similar situation; it was quite a struggle to pull out any of the individual folders from the alphabetical sections. I turned to my box files, twenty of them, each allocated to one or more specific subject. Here again they were crammed full. This shouldn't really have come as a surprise – after all, I have been a writer and broadcaster for about forty years, and anything which looked even remotely as though it might provide material for an article, a broadcast, or a titbit to hand out to the writers of *The Archers*, had been kept, just in case.

By far the biggest supply of material has come to me from listeners who over the past thirty years have been interested in the programmes on farming, gardening and country life that I have been responsible for over this period of time. Listeners to *The Archers*, particularly those who enjoyed Tom Forrest's introduction to the omnibus edition on Sunday mornings, provided a vast amount of material, much of which found its way into the programme. That material, and a lot more which did not quite fit the needs of the programme, was all amongst my filing and clogging up the system.

So, with grim determination to have a jolly good turn-out, I fetched a large square of hessian that I normally use to hold and carry away the grass cuttings from the lawn, and I spread this out on the office floor, pulled out the top drawer of the filing cabinet, and extracted the first folder in the 'A' section.

Right. All correspondence over three years old was to come out for a start. Of course, I couldn't just look at the date and discard it automatically – there might be something that I could still find a use for, and that is precisely what happened. The third letter I took out was from a gentleman called Abbot who had heard Tom Forrest talking about the kind of wood he liked to have for his fire, and he wondered if I would be interested in a poem he had found amongst his father's papers after he died. It was all about how the various sorts of wood behaved when the blocks were placed on the fire, and he enclosed a copy of the poem for me to see and hoped that one Sunday morning Tom would read it out. He did. Then I remembered that we had had so many requests from listeners for a copy of the poem that we had had to have dozens of copies made to send to them.

No, I can't throw that away. Might be useful again, you never know. But I had to make room. Oh, just that one won't make any difference. But it was quite hopeless. I found myself keeping more than I was throwing away. There was nothing for it but to keep one drawer in the cabinet specially for all the interesting letters, poems, proverbs, cures, recipes, country customs, folklore and the rest. I worked my way slowly through the hundreds of letters and masses of other papers and references and began to lay them out in sections and sub-sections, until there was hardly room on the floor to walk. At the end of the week I seemed to be knee-deep in paper – I was certainly going to need more than one drawer of the cabinet – and then the answer came: extract all the important bits and pieces and put them together in a book.

So began a task that has been a long, hard slog, but I must admit there were many nostalgic moments when I came across letters from people whose friendship I have enjoyed and valued, and odds and ends relating to the countryside which set me thinking about how they came into my possession. Many of these items I had completely forgotten – the margin of brown round the edges of many of the papers was a good guide to the length of time they had been around.

My in-tray is still spilling over, but now there is space in the filing cabinet, though I am sure there are going to be a lot more items that will have to be filed away, just in case.

So that is the reason for the following pages, and I hope they will give as much pleasure to others when they read them as they gave me when I sorted them all out.

Of course, I should really acknowledge my thanks to all the people who, over this long period of time, have provided me with so much material, but alas the list is far too long, and I can only hope if they happen to read the book and recall that they were responsible for bringing the item to my notice they will be happy to have made a contribution.

Few of my correspondents stated the source of their items, and although many claimed that they were local sayings or proverbs, I have since found many of them in Brewer's *Dictionary of Phrase and Fable*, and others in the county books published from time to time by the County Federations of the Women's Institutes. I am equally sure that many of the recipes and cures I received were originally collected and published by some worthy long since dead. Even the recipe book that had been the standby of a cook at one of the 'big houses' over a hundred years ago was no doubt laboriously copied out from a book that her mistress had supplied her with.

Over the years we have tried out many of the recipes and some have become firm favourites. As far as the cures are concerned, we certainly have not tried them all, but I am assured that many of the herbal cures are still in regular use today in some parts of the country.

In seeking to check a number of items I was glad of the confirmation and interesting details I was able to find in the following books: *British Calendar Customs* by A. R. Wright, edited by T. E. Lones, and published by the Folk-Lore Society, 3 vols., 1936–40; *The Lives of the Saints* by Omer Englebert, Thames and Hudson, 1951; *Flowers and Flower Lore* by the Rev. Hilderic Friend, Swan, Sonnenschein, Le Bas and Lowry, 1886; *The Language of Sport* by C. E. Hare, *Country Life*, 1939; *Traditional Recipes* by Nell Heaton, Faber and Faber, 1951; and *Farmhouse Fare*, collected and published by *Farmers' Weekly*. I want to say a particular thank you to the members of the County Federation of Women's Institutes in Merioneth for allowing me to draw freely from their collection of 'cures' that the members had collected as a project during 1973.

It has been very fascinating to me to discover among many of the old proverbs much that is applicable today. Even in this scientific age of farming, many of the reminders of dates, and sowing and harvesting times and procedures that our forebears worked out over many years' experience are just as applicable today as they were then. So, too, the weather lore. Many of the sayings of the past stand up to checking against the utterances of the modern weather forecasters.

Godfrey Baseley

February 1976

PART ONE

A Calendar of Saints' Days
and National Country Festivals

January

If Janiveer's calends be summerly gay,
'Twill be winterly weather to the calends of May.

The grass that grows in Janiveer
Grows no more all the year.

If one knew how good it were
To eat a pullet in Janiveer,
If he had twenty hens in the flock,
He'd leave but one to go with the cock.

As the days lengthen,
So does the cold strengthen.

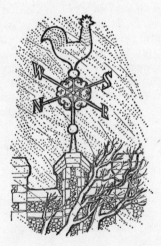

1st, NEW YEAR'S DAY

First footing. Letting in the New Year. The Scots have their own customs for greeting and toasting the first day of the year, but all over the rest of the British Isles the New Year should be greeted by a tall dark stranger who should enter the house with gifts symbolic of food, drink and warmth, and then pass right through the house. If the first-foot is a dark man, then the household will have good fortune for the rest of the coming year, but if, on the other hand, the first person to pass over the threshold is fair, or female, dark or fair, then ill fortune will follow.

If a bough of mistletoe is given to the first cow to calve after New Year's day the rest of the herd will be safeguarded from ill luck for the rest of the year.

5th, TWELFTH NIGHT

Twelfth Night is sometimes called Twelfth-day Eve, Old Christmas Eve or the Eve of the Epiphany. After the change from the Old to the New Style, certain districts continued, as far as possible, to keep their Christmas on 6 January, and to wassail their apple trees on 17 January, sometimes called Old Twelfth Night, or on 18 January, sometimes called Old Twelfth Day.

Twelfth Night is the start of the period when farmers used to wassail their orchards; this was believed to charm the trees which would result in a good crop the following season. Every district or county had its own specific date for carrying out this time-honoured procedure, which reached a peak around 17 January. Much lamb's wool (roasted apples, sugar, ginger, nutmeg, cinnamon, and wine and/or ale) was prepared for the wassail bowl, which was carried to the orchard where a toast was given and echoed by the assembled company in booming tones. The wording of the toast varied from place to place, but the following are typical:

Health to thee, good apple tree,
Whence thou may'st bud and whence thou may'st blow,
And whence thou may'st have apples enow.
Hats full, caps full,
Three bushel bags full
And my pockets full too.

Wassail the trees, that they may bear
Many a plum, and many a pear;
For more or less fruits they will bring
As you do give them wassailing.

Wassail, wassail all over the town,
Our toast is white, our ale is brown;
Our bowl is made of the maple tree,
We be good fellows all, I drink to thee.

After the toasting the remains of the wassail were poured over one of the trees in the orchard and a great shout was given to echo right through the orchard, or a gun was fired several times to drive away any evil spirits that might be lurking there.

Preparations for the revel of Twelfth Night included the making of a large and rich Twelfth Cake. A bean and a pea were inserted in the cake before baking and he who received the slice containing the bean was elected King of the Bean. She who received the slice containing the pea was elected Queen and they both enjoyed regal honours during the revel.

Another very old custom observed most popularly on Twelfth Night was the lighting of fires, which was done to bring success to the farm, dairy and orchard.

Christmas decorations are now usually left up until Twelfth Night, after which it is considered unlucky still to have them up, but in the past they were taken down on New Year's day, Plough Monday or Candlemas Eve. In some parts of Lancashire they were taken down to be used as fuel in making pancakes.

6th, EPIPHANY

The word Epiphany comes from a Greek word signifying manifestation or apparition. This day is sometimes called Old Christmas Day or Twelfth Day, and ceremonies like those of Twelfth Night were performed. Two centuries ago Twelfth Day used to be the most festive day of the twelve, especially in the north of England, and it was long the custom for the kings of England to attend, personally or by proxy, the Epiphany service at the Chapel Royal and offer gold, frankincense and myrrh in commemoration of the offerings of the Magi.

7th, ST DISTAFF'S DAY or ROCK (meaning distaff) DAY

This, the first week-day after the Epiphany and the conclusion of the Christmas festive season, was the day on which the women prepared to resume their spinning. The men amused themselves by burning the flax and tow used by the women, who, in turn, drenched the men with water.

Partly work and partly play
Ye must on S. Distaff's day.
From the plough soone free the teame,
Then come home and fother them.
If the Maides a-spinning goe,
Burn the flax, and fire the tow.
Bring in pailes of water then,
Let the Maides bewash the men.
Gives S. Distaff all the right,
Then bid Christmas sport good night;
And next morrow every one,
To his owne vocation.

Hesperides, Saint Distaff's Day, Robert Herrick, 1648

PLOUGH MONDAY – The first Monday after Epiphany

Plough Monday was the day for the men workers to return to their farm work after the Christmas festivities had ended and when the ground was neither too frozen nor too wet to commence ploughing. For many, however, Plough Monday was a festive day associated mainly with the Fool Plough Procession. This procession included a number of plough boys who, dressed as mummers, begged for 'plough money' which was used to buy provisions for a rustic feast and to buy candles for the maintenance of the ploughman's light which burned before the altar of the ploughmen's guild in a chantry of the church. In olden times, a plough, sometimes blessed and perfumed by the clergy, was included in the procession and was drawn by oxen, or, more often, by the plough boys who were then called 'plough bullocks'. The plough was rarely seen in the procession after 1875, however.

22nd, ST VINCENT

St Vincent was born in Huesca, Spain and died in 304. He was arrested when the persecutions of Diocletian began and died under torture.

In some places he is taken as patron by the wine-growers, but the reason for this patronage is not known, unless it be a pun on the first syllable of his name. St Vincent has also become known as the patron saint of drunkards.

> *If on St Vincent day the sky is clear,*
> *More wine than water will crown the year.*

> *Remember St Vincent day,*
> *If the sun his beams display;*
> *Be sure to mark the transient beam,*
> *For 'tis a token, bright and clear,*
> *Of prosperous weather all the year.*

25th, ST ANANIAS

Not very much is known about St Ananias. It is thought that he was bishop of Damascus and that he died by stoning in about 70 not far from his episcopal city.

When St Paul was blinded on the road to Damascus it was St Ananias who restored his sight and administered baptism to the former persecutor of the Christians.

St Ananias' day has sometimes been confused with St Paul's day due to the fact that St Paul's conversion took place on 25 January. St Paul's day is in fact 29 June.

February

Rain in February is worth as much as manure.

> *Much February snow*
> *A fine summer doth show.*

> *February fill dyke,*
> *Be it black or be it white;*
> *But if it be white, it is better to like.*

A warm day of February is a dream of April.

> *All the months in the year*
> *Curse a fair Februeer.*

1st, ST BRIDE

St Bride is known as St Brigid in Ireland, and also in the Isle of Man. She is thought to have been born in Louth or in Armagh about the year 450, and to have died about 520. She is one of the patrons of Ireland.

St Bride's day is also Candlemas Eve and used to be the time to take down Christmas decorations and replace them with box. If a leaf or a berry was found after this date, the member of the family who found it would die.

> *Down with the Rosemary and Baies,*
> *Down with the Mistletoe;*
> *Instead of Holly, now upraise*
> *The greener Box for show.*
> > *Hesperides, Ceremonies for Candlemas Eve*, Robert
> > Herrick, 1648

A traditional food to be eaten on this day was oat cakes.

2nd, CANDLEMAS

On Candlemas day throw candles away. (This is another reminder that the festivities associated with Christmas are over.)

Set beans in Candlemas waddle.

In olden times parishioners attended church on this day. Wax candles and tapers were consecrated, lighted, and distributed; they were then carried in procession to guard against evil spirits and storms. The bigger the candle and the more brightly it burned, the greater the protection.

This procession is one of the reasons Candlemas day is so called; the other is because lighted tapers, used all winter at vespers and litanies, were put away until the next All-Hallowmass.

Candlemas day is an important festival of the church, held in commemoration of the purification of the Virgin. It was particularly important to women, and used also to be called the Wives' Feast day.

In Scotland Candlemas day is the first quarter day, when payment of rents is due.

A farmer should, on Candlemas day,
Have half his corn and half his hay.

On Candlemas day, if the thorns hang a-drop,
Then you are sure of a good pea crop.

If the sun is bright on the day of Candlemas, there will be more frost after the feast than there has been before it.

When Candlemas day is fine and clear
A shepherd would rather see his wife on the bier.

If Candlemas be fair and clear,
We'll have two winters in one year.

If Candlemas be dry and fair,
The half of winter's gone or mair.
If Candlemas he wet and foul,
Half the winter's gone by Yule.

If Candlemas day be fair and bright,
Winter will have another flight;
If on Candlemas day it be shower and rain,
Winter is gone and will not come again.

When Candlemas day is come and gone,
The snow lieth on a hot stone.

14th, ST VALENTINE

On St Valentine's set thy hopper by mine. (This is a reminder to farmers that the sowing of spring crops should receive their attention.)

The feast of two saints called Valentine is celebrated on this day. Their stories are quite similar and have never been entirely clarified. One was a priest in Rome who is believed to have been arrested under Claudius the Goth and eventually decapitated on the Flaminian Way in about 269. The other is thought to have occupied the See of Terni in Umbria in about 223. He is said to have cured the son of a philosopher named Crato of an incurable disease.

When the prefect Abundius learned of this he had the bishop beheaded in about 273.

In medieval days it was believed that birds began to pair on 14 February, which is the origin of the custom of sending 'Valentines'.

> *Valentine's day is drawing near,*
> *And both the men and maids incline*
> *To choose them each a Valentine.*
>   Poor Robin's Almanack for 1757

The custom of giving Valentine buns, money, apples or oranges to children and old people varied in different places, but usually children would go from door to door on St Valentine's day and sing a few lines in order to obtain a gift. The following greetings are fairly typical:

> *Good morning, Valentine!*
> *Curl your locks as I do mine,*
> *Two before and three behind.*
> *Good morning, Valentine!*

> *Good morrow, Valentine;*
> *I be thine and thou be'st mine,*
> *So please give me a Valentine.*

On St Valentine's day every good goose will lay.

> *If she be a good goose, her dame well to pay,*
> *She will lay two eggs before St Valentine's day.*

A favourite food eaten on St Valentine's day was plum shuttles, or shittles, otherwise known simply as Valentine buns. These are dough buns, shaped like a weaver's shuttle, made with currants or caraway seeds.

24th, ST MATTHIAS

Little is known of St Matthias. In the first chapter of the Acts of Apostles Peter describes how Matthias was elected one of the apostles, to replace Judas. Some believe that St Matthias evangelized Palestine and suffered martyrdom there; others, that he preached the Gospel in Ethiopia and died in that country.

St Mathee sends the sap up the tree.

On St Mattio, take thy hopper and sow.

(The different dates under which similar proverbs concerned with operations on the farm appear above, and also those quoted for March, can be accounted for by weather and seasonal differences in the various parts of the country.)

SHROVE TUESDAY

This is the day the parish priest would hear confession from and give absolution to (shrive) his parishioners. The church bell would ring to call the faithful to church. After the Reformation the religious aspects of the day had begun to take second place to the more festive customs. The bell prompted the people to make pancakes, rather than to perform their religious duty.

> But hark, I hear the pancake bell,
> And fritters make a gallant smell;
> The cooks are baking, frying, boyling,
> Stewing, mincing, cutting, broyling,
> Carving, gormandising, roasting,
> Carbonading, cracking, slashing, toasting.
>   Poor Robin's Almanack for 1684

The tradition of eating pancakes on Shrove Tuesday dates back

many centuries; it is thought to derive from a kind of Pancake
Feast preceding Lent in the Greek Church.

> *Pit pat the pan's hot*
> *And I be come a-shroving;*
> *Cast the net before the fish,*
> *Something is better nor nothing.*
> *A piece of bread, a piece of cheese,*
> *A piece of apple dumpling;*
> *Up with the kettle and down with the pan,*
> *Give me a penny and I'll be gone!*
> *Give me another for my little brother,*
> *And we'll run home to Father and Mother.*

On Shrove Tuesday single girls would make a pancake and feed
it to the cock. The number of hens that joined him would be the
number of years before she would marry.

This day used also to be a popular day for cockfights.

ASH WEDNESDAY

The first day of Lent, which ends in forty days' time on Easter
day.

> *If you marry in Lent*
> *You will live to repent.*

Pudding pies are the traditional fare for Ash Wednesday.

It is customary for the clergy to burn and then bless the ashes
of the palms blessed on the Palm Sunday of the preceding year,
and to mark the ashes in the sign of the cross on the foreheads of
their parishioners. The ashes are a reminder that we come from
ashes and to ashes will return.

Jack O'Lent is a figure closely associated with Ash Wednesday.
He was made of pieces of wood or straw and dressed up in old
clothing. He was then paraded about and subjected to all kinds of
rough treatment. He was supposed to represent Judas Iscariot.

March

A dry March and a showery May portend a wholesome summer if there be a showery April in between.

So many mists in March, so many frosts in May.

If March borrows from April
Three days, and they be ill,
April borrows of March again
Three days of wind and rain.

March in Janiveer, Janiveer in March, I fear.

When it thunders in March, one must say alas.

A windy March foretells a fine May.

March comes in like a lion and goes out like a lamb; but, if it comes in like a lamb, it goes out like a lion.

March comes in with an adder's head and goes out with a peacock's tail.

A wet March makes a sad harvest.

March snow hurts the seed.

March dry, good rye.

A peck of March dust and a shower in May,
Makes the corn green and the meadows all gay.

March winds and April showers bring forth May flowers.

March dust to be sold is worth a ransom in gold.

The March wind causes dust and the wind blows it about.

The March sun raiseth, but dissolveth not.

March birds are best.

Mad as a March hare.

March search, April try,
May will prove whether you live or die.

1st, ST DAVID

Upon St David's day,
Put oats and barley in the clay.

St David is the patron saint of Wales, and founder of the See of St David. He died bishop of Menevia in 589.

It is customary for the Welsh to wear a leek on St David's day, and in London a popular ceremony is the presentation of leek emblems to the officers and men of the Welsh Guards.

Leek pie is the traditional dish for this day.

2nd, ST CHAD

St Chad was born in Northumbria and was a monk of the abbey of Melfton in Ireland before becoming abbot of the monastery of Lastingham in Yorkshire. He later became bishop of Lichfield, and died of the plague in Lastingham in about 672.

Before St Chad every goose lays, whether good or bad.

The goose used to be an important factor in the lives of cottagers and commoners. In the days when much of the countryside was open heath or 'common land', every habitation in an area where common land existed was allocated 'stints' or pasturing rights. These rights allowed the commoners to graze a specified number of geese (or other animal) on the common and unenclosed land, the number being determined by how many could be supported during the winter months on the enclosed land attached to their dwelling houses.

The rules and regulations associated with the rights of commoners vary in different parts of the country, even in adjoining parishes. In my own parish the stints are termed 'sheep pastures', but they can be used for horses and cattle in the following proportions: a right to two sheep pastures would allow the holder to graze one beast or one horse aged not more than two years. Three sheep pastures allowed for one milch cow or one horse not over three years of age. Five pastures allowed for a milch cow and either a beast or a horse not exceeding three years. To be able to put out a mare and foal it was necessary for the owner to hold seven pastures. One sheep pasture allowed for three geese.

In most country districts geese were allowed to graze free of restriction on specified parts of the common.

For many of the commoners, the sale of geese at Michaelmas provided them with the money to pay their rents, which were due this month.

12th, ST GREGORY

Pope Gregory the Great, patron of scholars, died in about 604. He sent Augustine and his monks, as Christian missionaries, to England, where St Gregory's day used to be remembered by husbandmen, who called 12 March 'Farmer's Day'.

17th, ST PATRICK

St Patrick, Bishop of Armagh and patron saint of Ireland, died about 461. The Irish, recently freed from Roman domination, were then ruled by a host of minor kings, and it was against these that St Patrick directed his zeal. The story of the evangelization of Ireland revolves round tales of the conversions he made.

Shamrock is traditionally worn by the Irish on this day, and in London the presentation of shamrock to the officers and men of the Irish Guards is a popular custom.

21st, ST BENEDICT

St Benedict, founder of western monarchism, was born in Norcia in Umbria about 480. He died of fever in 543.

This date is important in the fixing, for any year, of the date of Easter Sunday. Easter day falls on the Sunday following the fourteenth day of the calendar moon which happens on or next after 21 March.

On St Benedict's sow thy peas or keep them in the rick. (This is a reminder that any peas sown after this date may be a failure.)

25th, LADY DAY

The Annunciation of the Virgin Mary is commemorated on this day. It is also one of the quarter days in England when the payment of rents is due and when the commencement and termination of tenancies generally used to take place, and still does in certain parts of the country.

MID-LENT or MOTHERING SUNDAY

On Mothering Sunday, above all other,
Every child should dine with its mother.

Go a-mothering and find violets in the lane.

This is the fourth Sunday in Lent. The customs of Mothering Sunday are thought to derive from the ancient custom of parishioners going in procession to their Cathedral or other Mother Church on Mid-Lent Sunday to present their offerings.

Mothering Sunday was very widely observed in the country districts. When the majority of country children were put to 'service', i.e. engaged in either domestic or farm work, this was one of the very few holidays to which they were entitled.

The children would try to bring with them a nosegay of flowers that they had gathered on their way home along the lanes and across the fields. The traditional meal for their homecoming would be roast veal, followed by baked custard, with simnel cake and Mothering Sunday wafers served up for tea. (The word simnel comes from a Latin word, *simila*, signifying flour of the finest quality.)

Another traditional food on Mothering Sunday was frumenty, very nutritious and cheap to make. It is made of whole grains of wheat, parboiled in water, then boiled again in milk, sweetened with sugar, and flavoured with cinnamon and other spices.

April

April wet, good wheat.

April and May, key to the whole year.

April showers bring forth May flowers.

April weather, rain and sunshine both together.

An April flood carries away both the frog and her brood.

When April blows his horn, 'tis good for hay and corn.

A cold April brings both bread and wine.

After a cold April the barns will fill.

On the third of April come the cuckoo and the nightingale.

1st, ALL FOOLS' DAY

The first of April, some do say,
Is set apart for All Fools' Day,
But why the people call it so,
Nor I nor they themselves do know.
                    Poor Robin's Almanack for 1760

The above lines are as true today as they were in 1760, and the April-fooling custom is still celebrated.

Twelve o'clock is past and gone
And you're a fool for making me one.

If it thunders on All Fools' Day,
It brings good crops of corn and hay.

23rd ST GEORGE

St George is the patron saint of England, Portugal and Aragon. He was martyred in Lydda in Palestine in about 303 shortly after the accession of Emperor Constantine.

The most famous legend concerning St George is that in which he killed the dragon. The dragon lived in a lake near Silena in Libya and was appeased by being given two sheep every day. When the sheep became scarce it was offered maidens, who were chosen by lottery. The lot happened to fall to the king's daughter when George, a military tribune, was passing through the country. He killed the dragon at once with a blow of his lance.

The story of St George and the dragon is similar to those of Perseus and Beowulf, the killing of the dragon being symbolical, it is thought, of the triumph of noble ideals over those which are evil.

The Order of the Garter, the badge of which is the 'St George', was instituted by Edward III in 1348.

St George to borrow – by St George's day a farmer should be able to assess what his crops are likely to produce in terms of quantity, and on the basis of his assessment he could borrow with a fair amount of confidence that he would be able to repay. The lender, too, could judge the potential of the borrower's crops and lend accordingly.

24th, ST MARK

In Acts and Epistles St Mark the Evangelist is sometimes called John, by his Jewish name, and sometimes Mark, by his Greco-Roman name. He was St Barnabas's cousin and a native of Jerusalem. It is believed that St Mark composed his Gospel from the information he had from St Peter.

> *The Eve of St Mark by prediction is blest,*
> *Set therefore my hopes and my fears all to rest.*
> *Let me know my fate, whether weal or woe,*
> *Whether my rank is to be high or low;*
> *Whether to live single or to be a bride,*
> *And the destiny my star doth provide.*

PALM SUNDAY

This is the Sunday before Easter. It is sometimes called Fig Sunday due to an essentially Midland custom of eating figs and fig puddings on this day.

MAUNDY THURSDAY

This is the Thursday in Passion Week, sometimes called Shere Thursday or Holy Thursday, when the religious ceremony of washing the feet of others, especially inferiors, in commemoration of Christ's washing of His disciples' feet at the Last Supper, takes place. Edward II appears to have been the first English king to observe Maundy Thursday when he washed the feet of fifty poor men in 1326.

There are various theories as to the derivation of the word Maundy. Some think the word comes from *mandatum*, through the Old French *mandé*, meaning an order or command, others that it derives from *maund*, meaning a wicker basket with handles, which, it is said, was used for carrying the Maundy gifts. A third suggestion is that it comes from an old verb *maunder*, meaning to beg.

Shere (or Sheer or Chare) Thursday is a name for this day

which is thought to derive from the custom of shaving and cutting hair in preparation for Good Friday and Easter Sunday, though it could be taken to express cleanliness, which is, of course, closely associated with Maundy Thursday through the custom itself and the custom of cleaning altars on this day.

Maundy Thursday was in many parishes the day chosen to give alms to the poor or to deserving widows. The money came from established village or church charities, and was usually distributed from the church porch after a special service. In other cases the money had to be collected from the tomb of the benefactor to remind those receiving the gift of the donor.

GOOD FRIDAY

The name Good Friday probably derives from God's Friday.

On this day only really essential work was carried out, like feeding the livestock on the farms. After attending a service at the church, most countrymen would spend the rest of the day sowing and planting in their gardens. Good Friday was the acknowledged day for planting potatoes, because the Devil was supposed to have no power over the soil that day.

Hot cross buns are traditionally eaten on Good Friday. An old belief is that eating buns on Good Friday will protect the home from fire.

Until the time of Charles II a popular custom was to make rings for the fingers out of the handles or other parts of coffins, which, if consecrated on Good Friday, were believed to protect the wearer from cramp and fits. The consecration of these rings took place during a ceremony known as Creeping to the Cross, from which not even the king was exempt.

Another Easter feature of life in the past in rural areas was the custom of giving 'pace'-eggs. This worldwide custom dates back before the introduction of Christianity. Eggs were considered by the ancients to be emblems of the regeneration of mankind. Pace-eggs were hard-boiled and dyed various colours with logwood, onion skins, furze flowers and many other wild flowers and herbs. Red was the favourite colour, and this was supposed to allude to the blood of the Redemption. Names and sentiments were printed on the eggs and given to friends and neighbours.

The pace-eggs used to be blessed by the priest and the following benediction was in common use for the purpose: 'Bless, Lord, we beseech thee, this thy creature of eggs, that it may become a wholesome sustenance to thy faithful servants, eating it in thankfulness to Thee on account of the resurrection of the Lord.'

EASTER EVE

On Easter eve boys and men used to tour surrounding towns and villages and perform plays in order to obtain gifts – money, eggs, etc. This ceremony was known as pace-egging.

The next that steps in is old Miser Brown Bags,
For fear her money she goes in old rags.
She has gold, she has silver, all laid up in store,
She's come a-pasche-egging and hopes to get more.

EASTER SUNDAY

The word Easter is thought to derive from *oster*, to rise. Bede thought it derived from Eostre, goddess of the dawn and of spring, who was worshipped by the Anglo-Saxons about the time of the vernal equinox.

Easter is a movable festival, dependent upon the state of the moon. According to Haydon's *Dictionary of Dates*, 'Easter day is the Sunday following the fourteenth day of the calendar moon which happens upon or next after the 21st of March, so that if the said fourteenth day be a Sunday, Easter day is not that Sunday but the next.'

Easter day may be any Sunday of the five weeks which commence with 22 March and end with 25 April.

When Easter Day falls in Our Lady's lap,
Then let England beware a sad mishap.

The above saying warns that if Easter, representing our Lord, falls on Lady Day, England should beware.

At Easter let your clothes be new,
Or else, be sure, you will it rue.

After the short break for Mothering Sunday, Easter was the

33

first of the official holidays for the men and women in service at the big houses or on the farm.

The previous six weeks' fasting was eased on Easter Sunday and a wide range of meat, flavoured with many herbs, could be eaten. Tansy cakes and puddings used to be popular fare on this day, the bitterness of tansy being made more palatable by the use of ingredients such as cream, eggs, sugar, and lemon peel.

> *On Easter Sunday be the pudding seen,*
> *To which the tansy lends her sober green.*

A remarkable old custom on Easter Sunday was to journey early in the morning to a prominent point to see the sun dance. It was believed that the sun would dance for joy on this day in remembrance of the Resurrection.

EASTER MONDAY

Pace-egg rolling used to be a custom carried out by children on Easter Monday. A steep slope in some part of the parish was chosen for this event so that the eggs would roll down by their own momentum. The purpose of this custom has been lost, but no doubt it was at some time associated with a religious ceremony.

In many country parishes soul-cakes were specially made on Easter Monday to be given to the poor, who had to come and sing a song before being given a cake. The recipe for the cake has been lost, but the words of the song remain:

> *Soul! Soul! for a Soul cake!*
> *I pray you good missis, a Soul cake.*
> *An Apple, a Pear, a Plum or a Cherry,*
> *Or any good thing to make us all merry.*
> *One for Peter, one for Paul,*
> *Three for him that made us all.*

HOCKTIDE

The second Monday and Tuesday after Easter Sunday used to be the days when men and women went hocking, i.e. collecting money for the church, parish or various charities. The men usually collected on the Monday, the women on the Tuesday, which is generally called Hock Day. It is interesting to note, in view of the manner of collection, that churchwardens' accounts show that women were usually more successful in collecting money than men.

The method of collection was to tie up passers-by to enforce payment. The men would bind the women on the Monday, and the women did the same to men on the following day. After the Reformation, however, binding was prohibited for this purpose, and the practice then was to tie ropes or chains across the roads to stop passers-by and demand money.

'Heaving' was another custom, similar to hocking, which was carried out on these two days. On the Monday the men used to lift up three times over their heads any woman that they met. On the Tuesday the woman retaliated and did the same to the men. This custom was supposed in some way to be symbolic of the Resurrection.

May

Up merry Spring, and up the merry ring,
For Summer is acome unto day.
How happy are those little birds that merrily do sing
On the merry morning of May.

Who doffs his coat on a winter's day
Will gladly put it on in May.

Button to the chin till May be in.

Ne'er cast a clout till May be out.

A windy March and a rainy April make a beautiful May.

May makes or mars the wheat.

> *Mist in May, heat in June,*
> *Makes the harvest come right soon.*

> *Spud a thistle in May, it will come another day;*
> *Spud a thistle in June, it will come again soon;*
> *Spud a thistle in July, it will surely die.*

A hot May makes for a full churchyard.

Rain in May makes bread for the whole year.

Shear your sheep in May and shear them all away.

A dry May portends a wholesome summer.

Be sure of hay till the end of May.

> *Be it weal or be it woe,*
> *Beans should blow before May do go.*

A swarm of bees in May is worth a load of hay.

Flowers in May, good cocks of hay.

He who sows oats in May will have little to repay.

A leaky May and a dry June puts all in tune.

A May flood never did good.

A cold May and windy fills the barn finely.

> *He who bathes in May will soon be laid in clay;*
> *He who bathes in June will sing a merry tune;*
> *He who bathes in July will dance like a fly.*

He who would live for aye must eat sage in May.

If whitewashing is carried out during May a death will certainly follow.

People do say that only wantons marry in May.

Of the marriages in May the bairns decay.

Marry in May, repent alway.

May birds are always cheepin'.

1st, MAY DAY

Then while time serves, and we are but decaying,
Come, my Corinna, come, let's go a-Maying.
        Hesperides, Corinna's going a-Maying, Robert
                        Herrick, 1648

May Day has always been a great rural festival; the celebrations varied in detail from place to place, but basically there was little difference. It is the day when the Maypole was erected on the village green and the children danced round it holding the long ribbons that were attached to the top of the pole. The children were divided into two halves, one half dancing in the opposite direction to the other so that the ribbons became plaited as the dance progressed. When the ribbons were too short to allow the dancers to complete a circle, the dancers went into reverse and the plaiting was undone until the ribbons again hung free from the top of the Maypole.

A Queen of the May was chosen from among the girls, and it was her duty to take a garland of flowers or a hoop decked with flowers to the church, where it was placed on the screen and left there until the following May Day.

This pleasant custom used to be carried out with great pomp and ceremony and it was usually accompanied by a procession of Morris dancers and musicians.

In Elizabeth I's reign the Puritans began to abuse the Maypole and its votaries, and this hostility culminated in an Order being issued in 1644 to take down all Maypoles. After the Restoration the Maypole and Maypole ceremonies were again permitted, and Restoration day (29 May) became the popular day for the May Day celebrations. It was not until the latter half of the nineteenth century that the Maypole was again dressed on 1 May.

> *The fair maid who, the first of May,*
> *Goes to the fields at break of day*
> *And washes in dew from the hawthorn tree,*
> *Will ever after handsome be.*

Ill fortune comes to those who wash clothes on May Day.

ROGATION SUNDAY

This is the fifth Sunday after Easter and the Sunday before Ascension day. Rogation week is the week in which Ascension day falls, and this festival falls in May more often than in any other month. It is very much a rural festival, during which it was the custom for the clergy to go out into the fields and bless the crops.

ASCENSION DAY

In about 465 a series of earthquakes, storms, outbreaks of disease and incursions of wild beasts terrified the inhabitants of Western Europe. In order to restore some degree of morale, Mamertus, Bishop of Vienne, instituted a custom whereby rogations and supplications were made during ceremonial processions on Ascension day, or on one of the three preceding days. Litanies were chanted imploring divine protection. This custom was adopted in England early in the eighth century.

The Monday, Tuesday and Wednesday before Ascension day were called Rogation days, and sometimes Cross days because of the cross carried by the priest at the head of the procession. Later, these processions became disorderly, and at the Reformation they were prohibited, until Queen Elizabeth I's reign when the custom of 'walking the bounds' was introduced.

Queen Elizabeth directed that, 'In the Rogation daies of the procession they saye and singe in English the two Psalms beginning Benedic Anima Mea, with the litany and suffrages there-unto, with one homelye and thanksgiving to God already devised and divided into foure partes, without addition of any superstitious ceremonyes hereto-fore used.'

The elders of the parish, accompanied by the younger genera-tion, walked the boundaries of the parish, and at strategic points the boys were 'bumped' or 'whipped' with willow wands in order that they would not forget the position of the boundary. If, as was often the case, the line of a brook or stream marked the boundary, the boys were ducked in the water. There was another significant reason for these perambulations: to let the people in the neighbour-ing parishes know of the boundary lines and to stress that no encroachment beyond the line would be permitted.

In some parishes, where the land was flat, the children were taken to the top of the church tower on Ascension day to have the boundaries pointed out to them.

The deeds associated with all property these days, and the publication of Ordnance Survey maps, has made the custom of walking, or beating, the bounds unnecessary, but in the days of unenclosed commons and wide expanses of heath and open land such perambulations were of great importance.

Ascension day is still observed in a number of rural areas by the custom of 'well-dressing'. If a well or spring continued to run during a time of drought the people used to express their thanks on Ascension day by placing garlands of flowers beside it, and it is from this that the custom of dressing wells with flowers in the form of pictures is thought to originate.

WHITSUNTIDE SUNDAY

This festival falls on the seventh Sunday after Easter, and the week-days following make up Whitsuntide week. It is a festival observed in commemoration of the descent of the Holy Spirit upon the Apostles on the day of Pentecost.

'Whit' is generally thought to mean 'White'. Some think that this refers to the white garments worn by converts baptized on Whit Sunday, others that it refers to the old custom, observed on this day, of the rich giving milk from their cows to the poor.

For most people, particularly those in rural areas, Whitsuntide was a time for feasting and for frolics and games when Morris and country dancing were much in evidence.

This is also one of the quarter days in Scotland when payment of rents is due.

WHITSUNTIDE MONDAY

Whit Monday was the most popularly recognized day for the annual celebrations of the old village clubs when, with their banners and regalia, the members would walk in procession through the village to a field where they held their sports, games and trials of strength. Relics of these clubs are still to be found in a number of villages.

25th, ST URBAN

Urban I succeeded Pope Callistus I on 14 October 222. He died on 19 May 230.

Urban brings summer.

29th, OAK-APPLE DAY or RESTORATION DAY

This is the anniversary of Charles II's jubilant entry into Whitehall in 1660. This day is probably best known, however, for the events which gave it the name Oak-Apple Day, i.e. when Charles took refuge in an oak tree at Boscobel early in September 1651 while fleeing from Cromwellian troops after his defeat at the Battle of Worcester. The custom of wearing oak branches, twigs and leaves, and also oak galls or apples, became very popular; houses and horses were also decorated in this way.

After the Restoration the Maypole customs were celebrated in a number of countries on this day, instead of on 1 May. The first of May had become known as Ill or Evil May Day because of the abuses perpetrated by the Puritans during the May Day celebrations.

June

Calm weather in June sets all in tune.

A dripping June sets all in tune.

A leaky May and a dry June keep a poor man's head abune [in abundance].

A swarm of bees in June is worth a silver spoon.

A leak in June brings harvest soon.

Rain on 8 June foretells a wet harvest.

TRINITY SUNDAY

Trinity Sunday is a festival observed on the Sunday next after Whit Sunday in honour of the Trinity. It is thought by some that this festival was first introduced by Gregory IV in 834, but others believe its introduction was much later. Henry Wharton records that Archbishop Becket decided that Holy Trinity should be observed in England on the day on which he celebrated his first Mass, though it is said that about three hundred years earlier John XXII decreed that Holy Trinity be generally observed on the first Sunday after Whit Sunday.

CORPUS CHRISTI

Corpus Christi is the festival of the Blessed Sacrament or Body of Christ; it is celebrated on the Thursday after Trinity Sunday. It was instituted in the thirteenth century, in the diocese of Liége.

Before the Reformation the festival was celebrated in Britain by ceremonial processions and by pageants and plays on a grand scale. The main feature of the procession was the Host which was carried in an elaborately decorated pyx covered with a canopy of velvet. People bearing lighted torches led the procession, followed by the priests with the sacred pyx and then civic officers and members of the guilds. The processions were suppressed at the Reformation, though the pageants continued in certain areas.

11th, ST BARNABAS

Joseph Barnabas (meaning Son of Consolation) was a native of Cyprus. Most of what is known of him dates from the time he travelled with St Paul. Their apostolic work together continued for about four years. Tradition has it that St Barnabas died at Salamis, stoned and burned by Jews from Syria, in about 60.

Barnabas bright, Barnabas bright,
The longest day and the shortest night.

When St Barnabas smiles both night and day
Poor ragged robin blooms in the hay.

On St Barnabas'
Put the scythe to the grass.

15th, ST VITUS

Very little is known of St Vitus, also called St Guy. He was a martyr of the fourth century. He is considered to be the protector of epileptics and of people afflicted with chorea, the 'dance' which bears his name.

If St Vitus' day be rainy weather,
It will rain for forty days together.

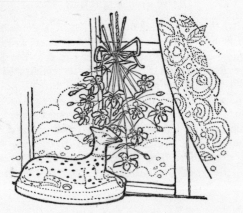

23rd, ST JOHN'S EVE or MIDSUMMER EVE

If St John's wort is gathered on the eve of St John's day and hung up near the door or window it will act as a protection against evil spirits and any dangers that may come with thunder.

Midsummer eve is a time for sun worship. An old custom on Midsummer eve was to light fires after nightfall or at midnight. These fires were called bonfires, a name which is thought to have originally been 'bonefires' because these fires used to be made up of bones. People would dance round the fires, and when they burned less fiercely they would leap through them. This was considered to bring good luck and protection from the evils of witchcraft. The custom dates back to ancient times and has close associations with the rites and beliefs of the Druids. These festival fires were prohibited by the Puritans.

The sowing of hempseed on Midsummer eve used to be a popular method for girls to divine who their future husbands would be.

> At eve last Midsummer no sleep I sought
> But to the field a bag of hempseed brought:
> I scattered round the seed on every side
> Then three times, in a trembling accent, cried—
> 'This hempseed with my virgin hand I sow,
> Who shall my true love be, the crop shall show.'
> I straight looked back and, if my eyes speak truth,
> With his keen scythe, behind me came the youth.
>
> 'The Spell', John Gay, 1714.

Another old custom was for people to sit all night on the porch of their local church on St John's eve to see the spectres of those who would die that year in the parish come and knock on the church door.

24th, ST JOHN or MIDSUMMER DAY

'I am . . . the voice of one crying in the wilderness,' said John the Baptist, 'Straighten out the way of the Lord . . .' 'Brood of vipers,' he said to the Pharisees, 'yield the acceptable fruit of repentance . . .'

St John spent the last part of his life a captive of Herod and he died the victim of a woman's vengeance. Devotion to him goes back to the fourth century; he has been set in the front rank of the saints by the various Christian churches. John the Baptist is the saint of whom Jesus said: 'There is no greater ... among all the sons of women.'

If the cuckoo sings after St John's day the harvest will be late.

Cut your thistles before St John,
You will have two instead of one.

Midsummer day is one of the quarter days in England, when rents are due.

29th, ST PETER

Simon, the son of Jona, lived in Bethsaida; before joining Christ St Peter was a disciple of St John the Baptist. He eventually became Bishop of Rome, where he was later crucified head downwards in 64 during Nero's persecutions.

Who praises St Peter doth not blame St Paul.

July

July to whom, the Dog Star in her train,
St James gives oysters and St Swithin rain.

If the first of July be rainy weather it will rain for full four weeks together.

The English winter ends in July and begins again in August.

A swarm of bees in July is not worth a butterfly.

15th, ST SWITHIN

Very little is known about St Swithin, or Swithun. He was an Anglo-Saxon bishop of Winchester from about 852 until he died in 861 or 862. Some have claimed that he wished to be buried outside the church so that he would be exposed to the feet of passers-by and the drops of falling rain; legend has it that when the cathedral in Winchester was completed in 971 and the bones of St Swithin were transferred from the churchyard to the shrine, the Saint protested and wept.

In some countries it was believed that if rain fell on St Swithin's day and 'christened' the apples this was a favourable omen. It was also thought that apples were unfit for food until after 15 July.

How, if on St Swithin's feast the Welkin lours [the sky threatens],
And every penthouse streams with hasty showers,
Twice twenty days shall clouds their fleeces drain,
And wash the pavements with incessant rain.

St Swithin's day, if thou dost rain,
For forty days it will remain;
St Swithin's day, if thou be fair,
For forty days 'twill rain nae mair.

25th, ST JAMES (the Greater)

This saint is known as St James the Greater to distinguish him from James the Less, 'brother' of the Lord, whose feast is on 1 May.

St James was, like St John the Evangelist, a son of Zebedee, and a fisherman. James and John were surnamed Boanerges, meaning 'sons of thunder', by Jesus when they wanted the fire of heaven to descend on a village which had refused to receive them. St James was the first apostle to die for Christ. While visiting Jerusalem with Peter to celebrate Easter in about 42 James was arrested and executed by Herod Agrippa.

Large quantities of oysters used to be eaten on St James's day. The children would make grottos out of the shells, illuminate them at night with rush lights, and ask passers-by for gifts or money.

He who eats oysters on St James's day will not want for money
during the year.

Till St James's day is past and gone,
There may be hops or there may be none.

August

Dry August and warm
Does harvest no harm.

A rainy August
Makes a hard bread crust.

HARVEST HOME

The Harvest Home Supper usually takes place in the farm's largest
barn; it celebrates the carrying home of the last harvest load or
the cutting of the last upstanding corn. Often part of the corn is
left standing to be cut ceremoniously and this corn is used to make
a figure which is dressed in white and decorated with coloured
ribbons. The figure is known as the Harvest Queen or Kern Doll
and is thought to represent Ceres, goddess of agriculture.

Often the upper parts of the stalks of the last upstanding corn
to be cut are tied together below the ears to form what is called a
'neck'. The neck is sent to any nearby farmer who has not yet
finished harvesting. This custom is called 'crying the neck'.

Harvest celebrations vary from place to place and the exact
time they take place obviously depends on the crops. The celebrations also include thanksgiving services for which the churches are
usually decorated with an appetizing display of the finest produce.

1st, LAMMAS

The word Lammas derives from 'loaf-mass'. This day used to be a
harvest festival when loaves of bread made from the new grain
were consecrated.

Lammas is one of the quarter days in Scotland, as it used to be,
but is no longer, in England.

A very old custom on this day concerned the rights of pasture common. Certain lands were used by their owners for growing wheat and other crops, but on Lammas day it was customary for these lands to be thrown open for use as common pasture and other purposes. The lands usually remained open until the following spring.

Gule is another name of 1 August, which is also known as the day of St Peter in Fetters.

After Lammas corn ripens as much by night as by day.

24th, ST BARTHOLOMEW

Very little is known about St Bartholomew. In the Synoptic Gospels and the Acts St Bartholomew's name is always mentioned with Philip's, and it is therefore probable that the two were good friends. It is thought that Bartholomew may be the same person as Nathanael, mentioned in the fourth Gospel.

If St Bartholomew's be fine and clear,
You may hope for a prosperous autumn that year.

St Bartholomew brings the cold dew.

All the tears St Swithin can cry,
St Barthelmy's mantle can wipe dry.

28th, ST AUGUSTINE

Aurelius Augustinus was born at Tagaste in Numidia in 354. He was instructed in Christianity, but he lost his faith in the course of his studies and from the age of sixteen led a life of sensuality.

In about 372 he formed a liaison with a woman which lasted twelve years, and he had a son by her named Adeodatus. He found his faith again in 386 and after Lent the following year he was baptized with Adeodatus by St Ambrose.

He became a priest of the church of Hippo in 391, and in 396 he replaced Bishop Valerius there.

Augustine died in 430 while the Vandals were besieging his episcopal city during those events which brought about the fall of the Roman Empire.

St Augustine is generally held to be the greatest doctor of Christianity.

A pot without bacon is like a sermon without St Augustine.

September

September blow soft
Till the fruits are in the loft.

September dries up wells and breaks down bridges.

14th, HOLY-ROOD or HOLY-CROSS

This is the festival of the Exaltation of the Cross. A popular custom on this day was to go nutting.

The Devil goes a-nutting on Holy-rood day.

21st, ST MATTHEW

Matthew, son of Alphaeus, had two names, as was customary among the Jews; he was also called Levi. He was a tax collector, one of the least honourable professions at that time. Christ's answer to the shocked reaction to his association with Matthew was: 'It is mercy that wins favour with me, not sacrifice. I have come to call sinners, not the just.'

It is not known how or where St Matthew died.

St Matthew shuts up the bees.

St Matthew brings the cold rain and dew.

> *St Matthew, get candle new,*
> *St Matthias, lay candlestick by.*

28th, ST MICHAEL'S EVE

The custom of cracking nuts in church used to take place on Michaelmas eve, but the meaning and origin of this custom remain obscure.

29th, ST MICHAEL

St Michael is one of the three archangels mentioned in Holy Scripture. The other two are St Gabriel and St Raphael. Michael was the object of a cult from the earliest Christian times. A church was built to him as early as the fourth century near Constantinople.

Michaelmas is one of the quarter days in England. It was long the custom for the landlord to hold his annual rent audit on this day and to provide a feast for all his tenants. This custom is still in being on many country estates, but the feast is now more likely to be held in the local hostelry than in the grand hall of the big house.

In the past, Michaelmas was the date for the termination of the year of service for the men and women hired at the 'hiring fairs' held the previous year who were anxious to make a change of master for any reason.

Popular fare for Michaelmas dinner was hot roast goose; this is the time of year when geese are in their prime.

And when the tenants come to pay their quarter's rent,
They bring some fowls at Midsummer, a dish of fish at Lent;
At Christmas a capon, at Michaelmas a goose,
And somewhat else at New Year's tide, for fear their lease
fly loose.
              Poems of George Gascoigne, 1552–77

On Michaelmas day the Devil puts his feet on blackberries.

October

It is unlucky to eat blackberries in October.

October blackberries are the Devil's.

Much rain in October, much wind in December.

For every fog in October, a snow in winter, heavy or light according to the fog.

If October brings much frost and wind, then January and February are mild.

> *A good October and a good blast*
> *To blow the hog, acorn and mast.*

Full moon in October without frost, no frost till full moon in November.

A warm October, a cold February.

If there is thunder in October, January will be wet.

If there is snow and frost in October, January will be mild.

Now that it is October, don thy woolly smock.

> *When chestnut leaves do fall,*
> *Cotton ain't no good at all.*

October always has twenty-one fine days.

If the October moon appears with the points of her crescent up, the month will be dry; if down, wet.

> *In October dung your field,*
> *And your land its wealth will yield.*

If during the fall of leaves in October many leaves remain hanging and wither on the bough, a frosty winter with much snow will follow.

If the oak wears its leaves in October you may expect a hard winter.

> *Fresh October brings the pheasant,*
> *Then to gather nuts is pleasant.*

If the deer's coat is grey in October there will be a severe winter.

If the hare wears a thick coat in October, then lay in a good stock of fuel.

If foxes bark much in October they are calling up a great fall of snow.

An October bride is fair of face and affectionate, but she is also jealous.

> *If in October you do marry,*
> *Love will come, but riches tarry.*

October was the principal month for the holding of fairs in the market towns and larger villages. The country folk from all around would bring their animals, which had been fattened up during the summer on the grass fields and commons, to be sold. Geese, cheese and any other items that were not required for the family were also sold at these fairs. Samples of grain from the current harvest were brought by the farmers to show to prospective buyers.

Most of these fairs were also 'hiring' fairs, or mops, to which farm workers would go to be hired for the coming year. In many cases girls and women who were looking for work in service would also attend in order to be hired.

When an arrangement had been made and a bargain struck with regard to wages, sometimes with the local bailiff in attendance, a small advance payment, usually a shilling (5p), would be made to enable the workers to enjoy the pleasures of the fair before going on to their new places of employment.

In some areas of the country, particularly in the Midlands, a 'run-away' mop would be held on a day in November so that the servants or farm workers who were dissatisfied with the conditions of their employment could try and find another job without having to wait a whole year. Martinmas, or Pack-rag day (see p. 57) was one such day.

18th, ST LUKE

'Beloved Luke, the physician' was the disciple, helper and friend of St Paul. He was a native of Antioch. His mother tongue was Greek, and he was the only one of the evangelists who was not a Jew. Luke is the author of the Acts of the Apostles and of the third Gospel.

He joined St Paul in about 50. He reached Macedonia in St Paul's company and then travelled with him to Philippi. Luke stayed in Philippi for some time while Paul continued his journeying alone. They met up again when Paul returned through Macedonia and they travelled together to Jerusalem where Paul was arrested in the temple. Luke stayed with Paul for the two years of his captivity, he was shipwrecked with Paul on the Maltese coast, and he never left him during his captivity in Rome.

Nothing is known of St Luke's last years and death.

On St Luke's day the oxen have leave to play.

St Luke was a saint and a physician, yet he is dead.

31st, HALLOW E'EN

This was the night that the spirits of the dead were supposed to appear. In certain parts of the country the custom was to light ceremonial fires on All Hallow E'en for the relief of souls in purgatory.

Hallow E'en was thought to be a favourite night for witches to make their appearance, and country folk, being very superstitious, would take every precaution to safeguard themselves and their animals from the evil influences of witches and witchcraft.

> *Hey-how for Hallow E'en*
> *When all the witches are to be seen,*
> *Some in black and some in green,*
> *Hey-how for Hallow E'en.*
> *Denham Tracts, 1895*

November

No leaves, no birds – November.

Ice in November brings mud in December.

> *If there be ice in November to bear a duck,*
> *There'll be nothing after but sludge and muck.*

A cold November, a warm Christmas.

> *On the first of November if the weather hold clear,*
> *An end of what sowing you do for this year.*

If the November goose bone [wishbone] be thick, so will the winter weather be.
If the November goose bone be thin, so will the winter weather be.

> *November's sky is chill and drear,*
> *November's leaf is red and sear.*

53

1st, ALL SAINTS

Hallow E'en, All Saints' day and All Soul's day are days devoted to thoughts of the dead, and the celebrations on all three days are thus related.

The celebrations on All Saints' day and All Souls' day had much in common. Festival fires were lit, church bells rung and souling and soul-cake customs carried out. Prayers for the dead are said on All Saints' day and commemorative services held on All Souls' day.

> *Remember the departed for holy Mary's sake,*
> *And of your charity, pray gi' us a big soul-cake.*

Children and adults would go 'a-souling' and beg for soul-cakes or any other gift. The words of the soul song were the same as, or similar to, those sung at Easter.

> *This night we come a-souling good nature to find,*
> *And we hope that you will remember it is soul-caking time.*
> *Christmas is coming and the goose is getting fat,*
> *Please put a penny in the old man's hat.*
> *If you haven't a penny a ha'penny will do,*
> *If you haven't a ha'penny a farthing will do,*
> *If you haven't a farthing, God bless you.*
>
> *You gentlemen of England, pray you now draw near*
> *To these few lines, and you soon shall hear*
> *Sweet melody of music all on this evening clear,*
> *For we are come a-souling for apples and strong beer.*
>
> *Step down into your cellar and see what you can find,*
> *If your barrels are not empty, we hope you will prove kind;*
> *We hope you will prove kind with your apples and strong beer,*
> *For we'll come no more a-souling until another year.*

2nd, ALL SOULS

In olden days All Souls' day used to be a solemn fast day. The souling and soul-cake customs mentioned above were celebrated on either All Saints' day or All Souls' day, depending on the traditions of different districts.

The term soul-cake could refer to anything given to a person souling. The actual soul-cake was usually flat and round, though sometimes shaped more like a bun or small loaf. They were usually light in texture and weight, rather like Madeira cake, and spiced. Milk and eggs were important ingredients.

5th, GUY FAWKES

This day commemorates the failure of the attempt by Guy Fawkes, Robert Catesby, Thomas Winter, Thomas Percy, John Wright and others to blow up king and parliament by gunpowder in 1605. Fireworks, bonfires and the burning of 'guys' are the main features of the 5 November celebrations.

> *Now boys with squibs and crackers play*
> *And bonfires' blaze turns night to day.*
> *Poor Robin's Almanack* for 1677

> *Remember, remember, the fifth of November,*
> *Gunpowder treason and plot;*
> *I see no reason why Gunpowder Treason*
> *Should ever be forgot.*
> *A stick and a stake*
> *For King George's sake*
> *Holla, boys, holla, make the town ring;*
> *Holla, boys, holla, boys, God save the King.*

Parkin and thar, or tharf, cake are traditional fare on Guy Fawkes' day. The ingredients for both are similar, consisting of oatmeal, butter and treacle, though ginger, baking powder and other modern ingredients have been added to parkin. Thar cake is thought by some to be a relic of an old feast, believed to have been held on 5 November, commemorating the Scandinavian god Thor.

9th, LORD MAYOR'S DAY

This is the day that the Lord Mayor of London is formally and ceremoniously installed in office. The chief attraction of this installation is the spectacular procession of the Lord Mayor and his retinue from the Guildhall to the Law Courts, and later to Westminster. This pageant first took place in 1215, and the title Lord Mayor is thought to have been introduced in the fourteenth century.

11th, ST MARTIN

St Martin of Tours was born at Sabaria in Pannonia in about 315. At fifteen he was enrolled in the imperial horse guards. When he was twenty he was baptized; he left the army and was made an exorcist by St Hilary at Poitiers.

In 371 he was carried off by force by the people of Tours, who were in need of a bishop. He remained there for twenty-six years during which time he travelled far and wide, converting many. He collapsed and died from exhaustion at Candes in 397. Martin became a very popular saint in the West, particularly in France where about four thousand churches are dedicated to him and over five hundred villages bear his name.

For centuries Martinmas was one of the most important days for the payment of rents, settlement of accounts, and the termination and commencement of tenancies. Except in Scotland, where Martinmas is still one of the quarter days, Christmas finally gained ascendancy over Martinmas as one of the four terms of the year.

This used to be a great day for feasting, drinking and merriment.

It is the day of Martilmasse,
Cuppes of ale should freelie passe;
What though Wynter has begunne
To push downe the summer sunne,

To oure fire we can betake
And enjoye the crackling brake,
Never heedinge Wynter's face
On the day of Martilmasse.

> *The Perennial Calendar and Companion to the*
> *Almanack*, Thomas Forster, 1824

Between Martinmas and Yule
Water's worth wine in any pule.

St Martin's little summer: at any time after Martinmas a short spell of fine warm weather can be expected.

Where the wind is on Martinmas eve, there it will remain for the rest of the winter.

Wind north-west at Martinmas, a severe winter to come.

Martinmas used often to be known as Pack-rag day, because St Martin's day, or a day near it, was a day when dissatisfied servants packed up their traps, slung them over their shoulders and left their masters and mistresses to find employment elsewhere.

23rd, ST CLEMENT

It is generally believed that Pope Clement was the third successor of St Peter and that he occupied the See of Rome during the last ten years of the first century. An old tradition which goes back to the fourth century says that he died a martyr in about 100.

Children used to visit their neighbours Clementing on this day; they would ask for money and food after singing or reciting verses.

Clemeny, Clemeny, year by year,
Some years apples and some years pears.
Butler, butler, fill the bowl;
If you fill it of the best,
God will send your soul to rest;
If you fill it of the small,
Down goes butler, bowl and all.

St Clement gives the winter.

25th, ST CATHERINE

St Catherine of Alexandria was the daughter of Costus, king of Cilicia, and Sabinella, a Samaritan princess. The period in which St Catherine lived is uncertain. She was baptized by the hermit Ananias. A ceremony known as 'the mystical marriage of St Catherine' took place after her baptism when the Virgin Mary appeared and placed a golden ring on Catherine's finger.

When St Catherine went to the emperor Maxentius to try and persuade him of the error of paganism she was imprisoned and died by torture.

She has been taken as patron by grinders, millers, spinners, wheelwrights and turners because of the spiked wheel which was used to torture the saint, and by scholars and philosophers because of her great learning. She is also esteemed as the patron of spinsters. Catherine-wheel fireworks are so named to commemorate the way she died.

This day used to be celebrated widely by feasting and merry-making, and children would sing songs and beg for gifts, a practice known as Catherning, or Catterning. Cattern cake used to be made to be eaten on this day.

> *Rise, Maids, rise,*
> *Bake your Catton Pies,*
> *Bake enough and bake no waste,*
> *And let the Bellman have a taste.*

At St Catherine's foul or fair, so it will be next Februair.

30th, ST ANDREW

St Andrew was a native of Bethsaida in Galilee; his name was Greek, however, and it signified 'courageous'. Like his father Jona and brother Simon Peter, Andrew was a fisherman and lived at Capernaum on the lake of Tiberius. He first met Jesus at Bethany where John was baptizing, but it wasn't until Jesus came to live and preach in Capernaum, after John had been imprisoned, that Andrew joined the apostolic group. It is thought that he died at Patras in Achaia on a cross in the shape of an X.

St Andrew is the patron saint of Scotland, and of fishermen

and fishmongers; barren women appeal to him also for children.

In lace-making counties in this country he has been adopted as patron of lace-makers, and St Andrew's day used to be a holiday for those involved in the industry.

> *St Andrew the King*
> *Three weeks and three days before Christmas comes in.*

ADVENT

This is the season including the four Sundays immediately preceding the festival of the Nativity. Advent Sunday is the nearest Sunday to St Andrew's day. For fourteen centuries Advent Sunday has begun the ecclesiastical year in the Western Church.

It used to be the custom for poor women to carry two dolls representing Christ and the Virgin Mary on this day, and every person to whom the images were shown was expected to give the bearer a halfpenny. It was thought unlucky not to have seen the Advent images before Christmas eve.

December

6th, ST NICHOLAS

St Nicholas was born at Patara in Lycia. He ruled a great monastery before being imprisoned for a time because of his faith. He died in about 324 as Bishop of Myra.

He is the patron and annual benefactor of children. He is said to have restored to life three children who had been murdered and hidden in a salting tub. This story, however, is thought to derive from the one concerning three girls whom he saved from prostitution by throwing them, at night, through their window, three bags of money. Some think the pawnbrokers' symbol of three golden balls originates from this. It is also an explanation of how the old custom of secretly giving presents on the eve of St Nicholas came about. The Santa Claus of Christmas derives from his name.

Another old custom on this day was the election of a boy bishop, usually a chorister of the cathedral. This custom goes back to the thirteenth century, but it was abolished by Queen Elizabeth I. The boy bishop used to remain in office until Holy Innocents' day, 28 December.

13th, ST LUCY

St Lucy is the patroness of Syracuse. She is believed to have suffered martyrdom in Syracuse during Diocletian's persecution. She vowed her virginity to God, and put off a suitor for three years. He revenged himself by denouncing her as a Christian, and when she refused to apostasize she was condemned to a house of ill repute. She eventually died by torture in about 303.

> *Lucy light, lucy light*
> *The shortest day and the longest night.*

20th, ST THOMAS'S EVE

Ghosts are free on St Thomas's eve and on the following days until Christmas eve.

21st, ST THOMAS 'DIDYMUS'

Little is known of St Thomas, the 'doubting apostle' who did not believe in the Resurrection until bidden by Christ to touch his wounds. He is mentioned specifically only by St John.

It is believed that after Pentecost Thomas went to evangelize the Parthians, Medes and Persians, travelling as far as India. He is sometimes represented with a square rule in his hand and is the patron saint of architects and masons.

House to house begging by poor women is the chief custom of St Thomas's day. Begging on this day was known as Thomasing, or 'going a-gooding'.

> *St Thomas grey, St Thomas grey.*
> *The longest night and the shortest day [this according to the 'new' calendar].*

If it freeze on St Thomas's day, the price of corn will fall; if it be mild, the price will rise.

Look at the weathercock on St Thomas's day; the wind will remain there for three months.

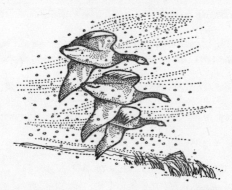

On St Thomas's night cut an apple in two and carefully count the number of seeds in each half. If the numbers are equal, then a marriage in the family will soon take place. If one of the seeds is damaged by the cutting the course of true love will not run smooth. If two of the seeds are damaged it denotes a widowhood.

24th, CHRISTMAS EVE

The Yule log is widely associated with this last day of preparation for the great Christian festival. A vast log was traditionally dragged to the kitchen heartstone, where it burnt throughout the festivities.

The Yule candle, or large mould-candle, was usually lighted at the same time as the Yule log and placed in the centre of the dinner table, where it had to remain without being moved or snuffed if evil was to be averted.

25th, CHRISTMAS DAY

At Christmas play and make good cheer,
For Christmas comes but once a year.

If the beech shows a large bud at Christmas a moist summer will probably follow.

A dull Christmas day with no sun bodes ill for the harvest.

A green Christmas brings a full churchyard.

A green Christmas brings a good harvest the following year.

If the sun shines through the apple trees on Christmas day,
When autumn comes they will a load of fruit display.

If ice bears before Christmas it won't bear a goose after.

Christmas day is an important quarter day in England.

26th, ST STEPHEN or BOXING DAY

This day commemorates the death by stoning of the first Christian martyr, St Stephen, in about 35. He belonged to that group of Hellenized Jews who had forgotten Hebrew because they remained abroad after the Babylonian captivity.

Bird shooting and wren and squirrel hunting used to be a popular activity on this day. It was also the custom to bleed livestock on St Stephen's day, which was thought to be good for the health of horses and other animals used for hard labour.

St Stephen's day is also known as Boxing Day due to an ancient custom of exchanging parcelled presents on this day.

Blessed be St Stephen, there's no fasting upon his even.

27th, ST JOHN

John was the son of Zebedee and Salome. He lived in Galilee, and like his brother, James the Greater, he was a fisherman. He was one of the St John the Baptist's disciples before he followed Christ. It was St John the Evangelist who was the first to recognize the risen Saviour on the shores of the lake of Tiberius.

By the end of the first century John was bishop of Ephesus. Tradition has it that he died in 101 aged over one hundred years.

St John to borrow – money used to be borrowed by farmers on this day to enable them to buy new seed for the coming crops. The farmer's stocks would enable the lender to judge the quality and quantity of produce the farmer was likely to have in the coming year.

28th, HOLY INNOCENTS' DAY

This day commemorates the children massacred by Herod's order. The festival was instituted in the fifth century; muffled church bells would toll and children were indulged to a greater extent than usual.

It was popularly believed that everything attempted on Holy Innocents' day, or Childermas, would go wrong.

31st, NEW YEAR'S EVE

Church bells ring in the New Year at midnight on New Year's eve, and people toast it in.

If on New Year's eve the wind blows south,
It betokeneth warmth and growth;
If west, much milk and fish in the sea,
If north, cold and storms there will be;
If west, the trees will bear much fruit,
If north-east, then flee it, man and beast.

PART TWO

The Weather and the Sky, the Days and Months, Years and Seasons

The Weather and the Sky

CLOUDS

Black snails indicate black clouds with much moisture.

Clouds on St Ananias's day [25 January] portend floods.

Clouds on the hills will come down to the mills.

One little cloud may hide all of the sun.

> *When clouds appear like rocks and towers,*
> *Earth's refreshed by frequent showers.*

When clouds are seen, wise men put on cloaks.

After black clouds, clear weather.

A cloudy morning bodes a fair afternoon.

If there were no clouds we should not enjoy the sun.

He that regardeth the clouds shall not reap.

FOG

A fog cannot be dispelled with a fan.

FROST

They must hunger in frost that will not work in heat.

The first and the last frosts are the worst.

After a frosty winter there will be a good fruit harvest.

A frost hurts not the weeds.

Walk slow in frost.

Frost and fraud both end in foul.

> *If the drop do freeze in the cup of the blum [bloom or blow],*
> *Surely there will be no plums.*

If bunches of nuts hang on the branches after the leaves fall, it betokens a frosty winter and much snow.

HAIL

Hail brings frost in its tail.

ICE

Ice in November to bear a duck, nothing to follow but sludge and muck.

If ice bears before Christmas, it won't bear a goose after.

LIGHTNING

When a house-leek grows on the roof of a house, that house will never be struck by lightning.

MIST

Mist in March, frost in May.

When the mist is from the hill,
Then good weather it doth spill [spoil].
When the mist is from the sea,
Then good weather it will be.

MOON

A light Christmas, light wheatsheaves;
A dark Christmas, heavy wheatsheaves.

A clear moon will bring a frost soon.

The full moon brings good weather.

It will be a wet month when there are two full moons in it.

Saturday new and Sunday full was never fine and never wool.

In the old of the moon a cloudy morning bodes a fair afternoon.

If after an indifferent new moon the third day is fine, the weather
will change for the better in its second quarter.

When the ring round the moon is far – rain is soon.
When the ring round the moon is near – rain is far away.

Friday's moon, come when it will, it comes too soon.

RAIN

A foot of rain will kill hay and grain.

Rain on Good Friday and Easter day, a good year for grass, a bad
year for hay.

A rainy Easter, a cheese year.

If it raineth when it doth flow,
Then take your ox and go to plough.
But if it raineth when it doth ebb,
Unyoke your oxen and go to bed.

If it rains with the flow, thee can go out to mow;
If it rains with the ebb, thee can go back to bed.

(The above two rhymes refer to areas near the sea or estuaries, the first specifically to the area around the River Severn.)

Many rains, many Rowans,
Many Rowans, many yauns [light crop].

If it should happen to rain three days together when the cuckoo sings among the oak trees, then late sowing will be as good as early sowing.

If a drop of rain or dew will hang on an oat at Midsummer there will be a good crop.

Rain before seven, fine before eleven.

When the dew is on the grass,
Rain will never come to pass.

If woollen fleeces spread the heavenly way,
Be sure no rain will disturb the summer day.

If the red pimpernel has its flowers fully opened first thing in the morning, no matter what the barometer may indicate, it will be safe to say that there will be no rain that day, and harvesting may proceed without fear. On the other hand, if the petals are still closed in the morning, then rain is on its way.

If St Vitus' day [15 June] be rainy weather,
It will rain for forty days together.

If July the first be rainy it will rain for four weeks.

St Swithin's day [15 July] if it do rain, for forty days it will remain.

Small rain can lay a great dust.

One already wet does not fear the rain.

In winter it rains everywhere, in summer where God chooses.

A poor man's rain cometh at night.

After rain comes fair weather.

If it rains well it will shine well.

All winds bring rain.

Although it rain, throw not away thy water pot.

For a morning rain leave not your journey.

A wet morning may turn to a dry afternoon.

To see rain is better than to be in it.

Small rain allays fear of rain.

Rain brings rest.

When it rains, it rains on all, just and unjust.

Many drops make a shower.

It never rains but it pours.

PORTENTS OF RAIN

If the down flies off dandelions, coltsfoot or thistles when there is
no wind, it is a sign of rain.

> *If the grass be dry at morning light,*
> *Look out for rain before the night.*

> *If red the sun before his race,*
> *Be sure the rain will fall apace.*

71

If the mountains are clear in the morning, there'll be fountains by evening.

If the petals of the red pimpernel are still closed in the morning, rain is on its way.

> *The hollow winds begin to blow;*
> *The clouds look black, the glass is low;*
> *The soot falls down, the spaniels sleep,*
> *And spiders from their cobwebs peep.*
> *Last night the sun went pale to bed;*
> *The moon in halos hid her head.*
> *The boding shepherd heaves a sigh,*
> *For, see, a rainbow spans the sky.*
> *The walls are damp, the ditches smell,*
> *Clos'd is the pink-eyed pimpernel.*
> *Hark! how the chairs and tables crack,*
> *Old Betty's joints are on the rack:*
> *Her corns with shooting pains torment her,*
> *And to her bed untimely send her.*
> *Loud quack the ducks, the sea fowl cry,*
> *The distant hills are looking nigh.*
> *How restless are the snorting swine!*
> *The busy flies disturb the kine.*
> *Low o'er the grass the swallow wings,*
> *The cricket too, how sharp he sings!*
> *Puss on the hearth, with velvet paws,*
> *Sits wiping o'er her whisker'd jaws;*
> *The smoke from chimneys right ascends,*
> *Then spreading, back to earth it bends.*
> *The wind unsteady veers around,*
> *Or settling in the South is found.*
> *Through the clear stream the fishes rise,*
> *And nimbly catch the incautious flies;*
> *The glow-worms num'rous, clear and bright,*
> *Illum'd the dewy hill last night.*
> *At dusk the squalid toad was seen,*
> *Like quadruped, stalk o'er the green;*
> *The whirling wind the dust obeys,*
> *And in the rapid eddy plays.*
> *The frog has chang'd his yellow vest,*

And in a russet coat is dressed.
The sky is green, the air is still,
The mellow blackbird's voice is shrill.
The dog, so alter'd is his taste,
Quits mutton bones on grass to feast.
Behold the rooks, how odd their flight,
They imitate the gliding kite,
And seem precipitate to fall,
As if they felt the piercing ball.
The tender colts on back do lie,
Nor heed the traveller passing by,
In fiery red the sun doth rise,
Then wades through clouds to mount the skies:
'Twill surely rain, we see't with sorrow,
No working in the fields tomorrow.

IT WILL RAIN IF:

Ducks, geese and other water fowl utter loud quacking sounds.

Pigs appear uneasy and rub themselves in dust.

Cattle and sheep collect in one corner of a field and turn their backs to the wind.

Autumn flies and gnats bite.

Frogs make a clamorous croaking.

Dogs become dull and sleepy.

Moles throw up more earth than usual.

Spiders are seen crawling on the walls more than usual.

Pigeons return slowly to their roosts.

RAINBOWS

If there be a rainbow in the eve,
It will rain and leave.
But if there be a rainbow on the morrow,
It will neither lend nor borrow.

Rainbow to windward, foul falls the day.
Rainbow to leeward, damp runs away.

SKY

Red sky at night, shepherd's delight.
Red sky in the morning, shepherd's warning.

If the sky should fall we should be able to catch larks.

From a cloudless sky a bolt may break.

A mackerel sky bain't long dry.

A mackerel sky, not wet, not dry.

Mackerel sky and mares' tails
Make lofty ships to carry low sails.

SNOW

Walk fast in snow,
In frost walk slow;
And still as you go,
Tread on your toe.

When frost and snow are both together,
Sit by the fire and spare shoe leather.

Snow that lies fattens the ground.

A snow year is a rich year.

Three feet of snow will make the hay and corn come more.

When you boil snow or pound it you only get water.

Snow is the poor farmer's muck.

SUN

The sun can only be seen by its own light.

He does not change country who always sees the sun.

He is very blind that cannot see the sun.

In every country the sun riseth in the morning.

When the sun is at its highest it casts least shadow.

While the sun shines nobody minds it, when eclipsed all consider it.

Make hay while the sun shines.

The sun is never the worse for shining on a dunghill.

The sun sees no difference between rich and poor.

> *If the sun in red should set,*
> *The next day surely will be wet.*
> *If the sun should set in grey.*
> *The next will be a rainy day.*

THUNDER

Thunder in spring the cold will bring.

When it thunders in March one may say alas.

When it thunders the thief may become honest.

Winter's thunder is summer's wonder.

Winter's thunder never boded good.

It never thunders but it rains.

Trefoil and clover will contract their leaves at the approach of a storm. Marigolds and wood sorrel behave in a similar manner.

Camomile flowers or St John's wort hung up in the house on St John's day [23 June] will provide protection against storms.

WEATHER

Cold and knaves come from the north.

Fair weather comes out of the north.

It is a pity fair weather should do any harm.

The good seaman is known in bad weather.

If it rains well it will shine well.

To a weak child all weather is cold.

What is good for plant is bad for peat.

> *If the cock moult before the hen,*
> *We shall have weather thick and thin.*
> *If the hen moult before the cock,*
> *We shall have weather hard as a block.*

> *If the oak is out before the ash,*
> *'Twill be a summer of set and splash.*
> *But if the ash is before the oak,*
> *'Twill be a summer of fire and smoke.*

THE WEATHER WILL BE FINE IF:

A raven is observed in the morning soaring round and round at a great height and making a hoarse croaking sound.

Swallows fly high.

Bats are observed to be flying about late in the evening.

Gossamer floats over the fields and hedges and goes out of sight.

Beetles fly about in the evening.

Dew lies plentifully on the grass in the evening.

THE WEATHER IS ABOUT TO CHANGE IF:

Dogs do much barking in the night.

The missel thrush is heard singing particularly loud.

WIND

God tempers the wind to the shorn lamb.

It is hard sailing where there is no wind.

The wind in one's face makes one wise.

The wind that will blow out a candle will help to kindle a fire.

A little wind kindles, much puts out the fire.

No weather be ill if the wind be still.

A southerly wind and a cloudy sky proclaimeth a hunting morning.

A straw will show which way the wind blows.

Take heed of wind that cometh in at a hole.

Wherever the wind is on Candlemas day [2 February], there it will stay till the end of May.

Wind on St Paul's day [29 June] indicates battle.

Where the wind is on St Thomas's day [21 December], there it will remain for three months.

Puff not against the wind.

He that pisses against the wind will wet himself.

You cannot catch the wind in a net.

Blow the wind never so fast, it will lower at the last.

Words and feathers are tossed by the wind.

The wind keeps not always in one quarter.

A windy year is an apple year.

He is about as much use as last year's wind.

> *When you see the gossamer flying,*
> *Then you'll be sure the air is drying.*

When the wind goes downhill it will be a duck's frost afore morning.

False birds can fetch the wind.

It's an ill wind that blows nobody good.

> *As true it is as a cow chews cud,*
> *And trees in spring do bring forth bud,*
> *Except wind stands as never it stood,*
> *It is an ill wind that turns not to good.*

The east wind is like a kite.

An east wind, like an old man, lies down in the sun.

> *When the wind is in the south,*
> *It blows the bait into the fish's mouth.*

When the north wind doth blow,
We shall have snow.

When the wind be in the north-west,
There'll be weather at its best.

When the wind is in the south,
Then the rain is in its mouth.
When the wind is in the east,
It's good for neither man nor beast.

The wind in the west suits everyone best.

The wind does not always blow from the west.

The Days and Months, Years
and Seasons

DAYS OF THE WEEK

Born on a Monday, fair of face,
Born on a Tuesday, full of God's grace.
Born on a Wednesday, merry and glad,
Born on a Thursday, sour and sad.
Born on a Friday, Godly given,
Born on a Saturday, work for your living.
Born on a Sunday, ne'er shall ye want,
So there ends the week and there's an end on't.

Monday's child is fair of face,
Tuesday's child is full of grace.
Wednesday's child is full of woe,
Thursday's child has far to go.
Friday's child is loving and giving,
Saturday's child works hard for his living.
The child that is born on the Sabbath day,
Is fair and wise, good and gay.

Cut them [nails] on Monday, cut them for health.
Cut them on Tuesday, cut them for wealth.
Cut them on Wednesday, cut them for news,
Cut them on Thursday, a pair of new shoes.
Cut them on Friday, cut them for sorrow,
Cut them on Saturday, see your true love tomorrow.
Cut them on Sunday, your safety seek,
The devil will have you the rest of the week.

Friday's dream, Saturday told,
Sure to come true, however old.

Friday flit, short time sit.

DAYS

The longest day must have its end.

As the days lengthen, so the storms strengthen.

TODAY AND TOMORROW

One today is worth two tomorrows.

Today is yesterday's pulpit.

Rather an egg today than a possible hen tomorrow.

Never put off till tomorrow what can be done today.

Live for today, not for tomorrow.

Today must borrow nothing from tomorrow.

When God says today, the Devil says tomorrow.

Leave tomorrow till tomorrow.

Life put off till tomorrow is too late.

Tomorrow never comes.

No one has ever seen tomorrow.

MORNING

When the morn riseth red,
Rise not thou, but keep thy bed.

EVENING

In the evening the idle man begins to get busy.

They had never an ill day that had a good evening.

NIGHT

Most men are begotten in the night.

A blustering night can lead to a fair day.

What is done under the cover of night is seen in the day.

He that runs at night may well fall.

The night is the mother of good council.

MONTHS

One month is nothing without the others.

Thirty days hath September, April, June and November,
All the rest have thirty-one, excepting February alone,
Which hath but twenty-eight days clear,
And twenty-nine in each leap year.

YEARS

Make plans for the year at the beginning.

Speak no ill of the year till it is gone.

A year does nothing but begin and end.

The year borrows another year's food.

Each passing year robs us of something.

A new year comes only once in a twelve-month.

He that lives not well one year sorrows seven after.

SPRING

Spring is the slayer of winter.

Spring has come when you can put a foot on three daisies.

In spring heat returns to the house.

SUMMER

Summer goes with the swallows.

Urban [25 May] gives summer.

A dry summer ne'er made a dear peck.

Do what you will, summer hath its flies.

AUTUMN

There can be no autumn fruit without spring blossoms.

Of all fair things, the autumn is fair.

Autumn gives us fruit; summer is comely with crops; spring supplies us with flowers; winter is alleviated by fire.

WINTER

A fair day in winter is the mother of a storm.

A good winter, a good summer.

A green winter, a fat churchyard.

After a frosty winter there will be a good fruit harvest.

It is a hard winter when wolf eats wolf.

In winter it rains everywhere, in summer, where God chooses.

Winter is summer's heir.

Winter never rots in the sky.

Winter's thunder and summer's flood never boded Englishmen good.

Winter thunder, summer's hunger.

One fair day in winter makes not birds merry.

There is winter enough for the snipe and the woodcock too.

He that passes a winter's day escapes an enemy.

What summer gets, winter eats.

Every mile is two in winter.

PART THREE

Farming: the Land, its Produce, Occupants and Utensils

Farming etc.

Better to follow a sloven than a scientific farmer.

Farmers fatten most when famine reigns.

Our farmers round, well pleased with constant gain,
Like other farmers, flourish and complain.

Cuckoo oats and woodcock hay make the farmer run away.

Good husbandry is good divinity.

Praise the great farmer, cultivate the small.

A farmer prefers a stout thistle to a red poppy.

'Tis the farmer's care that makes the field bear.

The foot of the farmer manures the field.

He that by the plough would thrive must either hold or drive.

A bad farmer's hedge is full of gaps.

To break a pasture will make a man,
To make a pasture will break a man.

Each man reaps his own farm.

So many hours must I tend my flock;
So many hours must I take my rest;
So many hours must I contemplate;
So many hours must I sport myself;
So many days my eyes have with young;
So many weeks ere the poor fools will ean;
So many months ere I shall shear the fleece;
So many minutes, hours, days, months and years,
Passed over to the end they were created,
Would bring white hairs unto a quiet grave.

A FARMER'S TOAST

Let the wealthy and great
Roll in splendour and state,
I envy them not, I declare it.
I eat my own lamb,
My chickens and ham,
I shear my own fleece and I wear it.
I have lawns, I have bowers,
I have fruits, I have flowers,
The lark is my morning's alarmer.
So joyfully boys now,
Here's God speed the plough,
Long life and success to the farmer!

BARLEY

When the sloe tree is as white as a sheet, sow your barley whether it is fine or wet.

It is ill prizing the green barley.

BEANS

Be it weal or be it woe,
Beans blow before May doth go.

When beans are in flower, fools are in power.

Every bean has its black.

Shake a Leicestershire man and you will hear beans rattle.

Sow beans in mud and they will grow like wood.

Sow beans in Candlemas waddle.

He has gone into the bean field [i.e. he is asleep].

CARTS

The worst spoke in the wheel of a cart will break first.

A creaky cart goes long on its wheels.

Keep the rake near the scythe, and the cart near the rake.

CORN

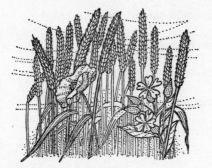

You may know by a handful the whole sack.

After Lammas [1 August] corn ripens as much by night as by day.

Corn and horn go together.

In good years corn is hay; in ill years straw is corn.

The heaviest ear of corn bends lowest.

Look at corn in May and you will come weeping away;
Look at corn in June and you will sing another tune.

No corn without chaff.

Sow corn in clay, wheat in dirt, and rye in dust.

When you grind corn, give not flour to the Devil and bran to God.

Much corn can lie under the straw.

Good corn is not reaped from a bad field.

FIELDS

A crop seems more abundant in another's field.

Fields have eyes, woods have ears.

If fields are prisons, where is liberty?

A little field can grow good corn.

Out of old fields comes new corn.

Good corn is not gathered from bad fields.

Happy is he that farms the fields of his fathers.

FLOCKS

The flock follows the bell wether [castrated male sheep who has a bell tied round his neck to enable the shepherd to locate his flock].

GRASS

Grass grows not on a busy roadway.

Soon grass, soon hay.

While grass grows the steed starves.

Grass grows at last above all graves.

He has gone to grass with his teeth upwards [i.e. he is dead and buried].

The grass is always greener on the other side of the fence.

HARVEST

Good harvests make men prodigal; bad, provident.

A man should live within his harvest.

He that hath a good harvest must be content to have some thistles.

Harvest comes not every day, though it comes once every year.

When the corn is ripe, it is time to reap.

He's as welcome as snow in harvest.

HAY

Be sure of hay till the end of May.

Rain on Good Friday and Easter Day, a bad year for hay.

Make hay while the sun shines.

The first cock of hay frightens the cuckoo away.

Flowers in May, fine cocks of hay.

HEDGES

A low hedge is easy to leap.

A hedge between keeps friendships green.

One thorn bush does not make a hedge.

LAND

Make not ridges on good land.

Good land, bad travelling.

Half an acre of land is good land.

He that buys land also buys stones.

Lime makes a rich father but a poor son.

A man's worth is the worth of his land.

MEADOWS

A thin meadow is soon mowed.

The scythe feeds the meadow.

OATS

If a drop of rain or dew will hang on an oat at Midsummer, there will be a good crop.

Oats will mow themselves.

He is sowing his wild oats.

ORCHARDS

An orchard is easy to rob when no one keeps it.

PLOUGHS, PLOUGHING AND PLOUGHMEN

He that counts all costs will never put plough to the ground.

Plough deep while sluggards sleep.

A man must plough with such oxen as he hath.

One man ploughs, another sows; who reaps, no one knows.

A ploughman on his legs is higher than a king on his knees.

There belongs more to a ploughman than his whistle.

A plough that works, shines.

It is folly to try to put the plough in front of the oxen.

POACHERS

A poacher is a keeper turned inside out.

A thief of venison makes the best forest keeper.

Old poachers make good gamekeepers.

POTATOES

Plant potatoes on Maundy Thursday, turnips on St Margaret's day [20 July].

The lazy man would have his potatoes grow at the potside.

It is no use planting cooked potatoes.

RYE

March dry, good rye;
April wet, good wheat.

SACKS

A full sack raises its ear.

A full sack will take a clout on its side.

An old sack needs much patching.

It is a bad sack that cannot be patched.

Fasten the sack before it is too full.

A torn sack will hold little corn.

Nothing came out of a sack but what went in it.

SADDLES

A saddle fits more backs than one.

Be sure to put the saddle on the right horse.

He that eats on his own must saddle his own horse.

SEEDS

Plant your seeds in a row,
One for pheasant, one for crow,
One to eat and one to grow.

SOIL

Let your strongest oxen plough your richest soil.

Noble plants suit not stubborn soil.

The richest soil, uncultivated, produces the rankest weeds.

Lime makes a rich father, but a poor son.

SOWING

The busy brain that sows not corn, sows thistles.

Early sow, early mow.

Forbear not sowing because of birds.

Sow dry and set in the wet.

Sow wheat in dirt and rye in dust.

Sow beans in mud and corn in clay.

St Matto [24 February], take hopper and sow.

He who sows on the highway loses his corn.

He who sows thorns should not go barefoot.

Sow barley when the sloe is white.

If it should happen to rain three days together when the cuckoo sings among the oak trees, then late sowing will be as good as early sowing.

STRAW

Straw is corn in a bad year.

They stumble at a straw but leap over a block.

That's the straw that broke the camel's back.

Many straws may bind an elephant.

Throw a straw to see which way the wind blows.

Let an ill man lay in your straw and he will look to be your heir.

He that hath skirts of straw should fear the fire.

THISTLES

Thistles are salads for goats and asses.

> *If you cut your thistles before St John [23 June],*
> *You will have two instead of one.*

Thistles and thorns prick sore, but evil tongues prick more.

> *Spud a thistle in May, it will come another day.*
> *Spud a thistle in June, it will come again soon.*
> *Spud a thistle in July and it will surely die.*

THORNS

Thorns come forth with point forward.

He who sows thorns should not go barefoot.

He that handles thorns must surely prick his finger.

TURNIPS

The best of the turnip is underground.

You cannot get blood out of a turnip.

WAGGONS

An empty waggon shall make way for a full one.

The waggon goes where the horse doth draw it.

Empty waggons make most noise.

WEEDS

Ill weeds grow apace.

The worst weeds flourish fastest.

One ill weed mars a pot of pottage.

The weed on a dunghill lifts his head highest.

Weeds need no sowing.

The good garden may have a foul weed.

The frost hurts no weeds.

One year's seeding makes seven years' weeding.

WOOL

It is better to give the wool than the sheep.

It is an ill wool that will take no dye.

Many go out to gather wool and come home shorn.

PART FOUR

Creatures

Mammals

ASSES

An ass is but an ass, though he be laden with gold.

The ass that carries wine drinks water.

Asses fetch provender, horses eat it.

Better to ride an ass that will carry you than a horse that will throw you.

A live ass is worth more than a dead horse.

Do not tie up asses with horses.

Every ass likes to hear himself bray.

Every ass thinks himself worthy to stand with the king's horses.

It is best to hold an ass by the bridle.

Asses that bray most eat least.

A hungry ass will eat any straw.

Give an ass oats and he runs after thistles.

It is other people's burdens that kill an ass.

Two proud men cannot ride one ass.

When an ass climbs a ladder we may find wisdom in women.

CALVES

A new-born calf does not fear a tiger.

A quiet calf sucks its own dam and another.

CATS

Thanks will not feed the cat.

In the dark all cats are grey.

A cat is honest when the meat is on the hook.

A scalded cat fears cold water.

An old cat laps as much as a kitten.

An old cat sports not with its prey.

When the cat and the mouse agree, the farm has no chance.

Keep no more cats than will eat mice.

A cat in gloves will never catch a mouse.

A mewing cat is never a good mouser.

He who hunts with cats will only catch mice.

What can you have of a cat but her skin?

Parliament is like a cat, cursed with age.

The cat loves fish, but dare not wet her paws.

A cat has nine lives.

COLTS

The wildest colts make the best horses.

A ragged colt may make a good horse.

Even a good colt needs breaking.

You may break a colt, but not an old horse.

It is a good colt that will break its halter.

A colt is worth nothing unless it breaks its cord.

COWS

A bletherin' cow soon forgets her calf.

A curst cow hath short horns.

If you sell a cow you sell the milk.

A good cow can have a bad calf.

All is not butter that comes from a cow.

A dead cow gives no milk.

What is the use of a cow that gives plenty of milk, but kicks over the pail?

A cow knows the worth of her tail.

Dairy farming is being tied to a cow's tail.

DOGS

A good dog does not bark without cause.

A lean dog shames its master.

A living dog is better than a dead lion.

All are not thieves that dogs bark at.

An old dog does not bark for nothing.

Barking dogs seldom bite.

Cowardly dogs bark loudest.

Dogs that are fierce in the woods are quiet at home.

A beaten dog is afraid of the stick's shadow.

A curst cur must be tied short.

Why keep a dog and bark yourself?

A dog that fetches will carry.

The foremost dog catches the hare.

In the kitchen the dog desires no company.

Let sleeping dogs lie.

One dog barks at something and the others bark at him.

The dog that puts up many hares kills none.

Sleep with a dog and rise with fleas.

Any stick will beat a dog.

One dog can drive a flock of sheep.

Trust not a dog that licks the ashes.

A little dog can start a hare.

We may not expect a good whelp from a bad dog.

Every dog hath his day, every man his hour.

A dog on his own dunghill is bold.

Beware a silent dog and still water.

A bad dog never sees the wolf.

In the mouth of a bad dog often falls a good bone.

A scalded dog fears cold water.

Better a dog fawn on you than bite you.

When the dog comes a stone cannot be found; when the stone is found the dog does not come.

You cannot teach old dogs new tricks.

Dog does not eat dog.

Give a child his will, and a dog his fill, and neither will do well.

Give a dog a bad name and hang him.

The dog gnaws a bone because he cannot swallow it.

A good dog deserves a good bone.

A good dog never barketh about a bone.

It is an ill dog that deserves not a crust.

Let people talk and dogs bark.

A man may cause his own dog to bite him.

There are more ways of killing a dog than by hanging.

There is no dog so sad that he will not wag his tail.

An old dog biteth sore.

An old dog cannot alter his way of barking.

If the old dog barks, he gives council.

A dog's life: hunger and ease.

He sleeps as dogs do, as wives talk.

A well-bred dog goes out when he sees you are preparing to kick him.

What servant is more attached to his master than his dog?

Dainty dogs may eat dirty puddings.

Dead dogs don't bite.

Dogs that hunt foulest scent the most faults.

Modest dogs miss much meat.

While dogs snarl at each other the wolf steals the sheep.

Women and dogs set men together by the ears.

One ought to take heed of an old dog's bark.

Trust not a horse's hoof or a dog's tooth.

Two dogs strive for a bone, and the third runs away with it.

He that hath a mind to beat a dog will easily find a stick.

DONKEYS

If you cannot drive an ox, drive a donkey.

He is like a donkey between two bundles of hay.

Short and sweet, like a donkey's gallop.

> *When a donkey starts to bray,*
> *It's time to cock your corn and hay.*

FOXES

A fox might change his skin, but not his manners.

He that would deceive a fox must rise betimes.

If foxes bark much in October, they are calling up a great fall of snow.

A fox is not taken twice in the same snare.

An old fox is hardly caught in a snare.

An old fox need not be taught tricks.

A fox runs as long as he has fear.

A fox fares best when he is most curst.

A fox knows much, but more he that catcheth him.

A fox never dies in his own dirt.

Like a fox, grey before he is good.

A fox should be hunted like a gentleman.

When the fox preaches, take care of the geese.

Forsake not the market for the fox.

There is many a fox hunted that is not killed.

At length the fox turns monk.

Though the fox run, the chicken hath wings.

A fox never speeds better than when he is on his own errand.

Let every fox look after his own brush.

Every fox looks after his own skin.

FROGS

The frog's own croak betrays him.

Even a frog would bite if it had teeth.

Though boys throw stones at frogs in sport, frogs do not die in sport, but in earnest.

HARES

If you run after two hares you will catch neither.

God sent readier meat than a running hare.

Hares are not caught with drums.

First catch your hare, then cook it.

Hares may pull dead lions by the beard.

If the hare wears a thick coat in October, lay in a good stock of fuel.

He runs with the hare and hunts with the hounds.

Little dogs start the hare and the great ones get her.

Where we least think, there goeth the hare away.

HORSES

A cough will stay longer by a horse than a peck of oats.

A golden bit does not make a horse any better.

You cannot judge a horse by its harness.

A horse is neither better nor worse for his trappings.

Don't look a gift-horse in the mouth.

A good horse cannot be a bad colour.

Even a good horse may need a spur.

A grunting horse seldom fails his master.

Never change horses in the middle of a stream.

It is better to lose a saddle than a horse.

Better to ride an ass that will carry you than a horse that will throw you.

It is not enough to learn to ride, one must also learn to fall.

He who never rode never fell.

A horse's ear is in his bridled mouth.

Let the best horse leap the hedge first.

Nothing fattens a horse so much as his master's eye.

He that would have luck with horses should kiss the parson's wife.

The wildest colts make the best horses.

Let a horse drink when he will, not what he will.

A good horse never lacks a saddle.

A man is not a horse because he was born in a stable.

He has been bitten by a brewer's horse [i.e. he is drunk].

A horse with one white foot, keep him to the end.

> *One white leg, buy a horse;*
> *Two white legs, try a horse;*
> *Three white legs, shy a horse;*
> *Four white legs, shoot a horse.*

A hungry horse makes a clean manger.

You can lead a horse to water but you cannot make him drink.

It is a proud horse that will not carry its own provender.

Anybody can cure a kicking horse but he that has it.

LAMBS

Rise with the lark and go to bed with the lamb.

A pet lamb makes a cross ram.

He that hath one lamb makes it fat.

She is mutton dressed up as lamb.

Make yourself into a lamb and the wolves will eat you.

A ewe that will not hear her lamb when it baas will never hear **a** calf when it bleats.

MICE

As hungry as a church mouse.

Better a mouse in the pot than no flesh at all.

A dead mouse feels no cold.

The escaped mouse never knows the taste of the bait.

It is a bold mouse that shares the cat's bed.

When the cat's away the mice do play.

Mice do not play with the cat's son.

The mouse should not try to cast a shadow like an elephant.

It is a poor mouse that sits on a meal sack and does not eat.

As merry as mice in malt.

MOLES

A mole needs no lantern.

OXEN

An old ox makes a straight furrow.

The tired ox treads surest.

God gives short horns to savage oxen.

Old oxen have stiff horns.

The ox lies still while the geese are hissing.

Take heed of an ox in front, an ass behind, and a monk on all sides.

Where no oxen are the crib is clean.

He who greases the cart wheels helps the oxen.

If an ox fall, whet your knife.

Beauty draws more than oxen.

PIGS and HOGS

A barren sow is never good to pigs.

A pretty pig makes an ugly old sow.

An alewife's pig is always well fed.

As a sow fills, the pigwash lessens.

Better a pig come dirty home than not return.

The first pig in the litter is the best.

He does not lose his alms who gives it to his pigs.

Feed a pig and you will have a hog.

Little pigs eat large potatoes.

Pigs grow fat where lambs would starve.

Pigs grunt about everything and nothing.

Pigs will prosper that lie close together.

The cunning pig eats the draff, the mad one rushes by it.

Swine, women and bees are hard to turn back.

A young pig can grunt like an old sow.

It is a lazy pig that will not eat ripe pears.

Poor and pert, like the parson's pig.

Old pigs have hard snouts.

Like a hog, he does no good till he dies.

A hog is never good till he is on the dish.

A hog prefers bran to roses.

A dirty hog is better than none.

He that has one hog makes him fat.

Everybody basteth a fat hog.

SHEEP

It is better to be a shrew than a sheep.

It is better to give the wool than the sheep.

Every baa loses a bite.

Good pastures make good sheep.

A lone sheep is in danger from a wolf.

One scabbed sheep will spoil the flock.

Shear your sheep in May and shear them all away.

There is a black sheep in every fold.

As well be hanged for a sheep as a lamb.

If one sheep leads over the dyke the rest will follow.

A good shepherd shears his sheep, he doesn't flay them.

Seven shepherds spoil a flock.

Valley sheep are fattest.

WEASELS

You can never catch a weasel asleep.

When the weasel and the cat marry, it bodes ill.

WOLVES

The death of the wolf is the safety of the sheep.

If you cut down the woods you will see a wolf.

Ill herds make fat wolves.

If you live with a wolf you will learn to howl.

To tame a wolf you must marry him.

Wake not a sleeping wolf.

A wolf knows what the ill beast thinks.

Wolves lose teeth, but not memory.

When a wolf grows old, a crow may ride on him.

COLLECTIVE NOUNS OF ANIMALS

Animals (any collection of): menagerie
Asses: pace, herd or drove
Bloodhounds: sute
Cats: clouder or cluster; kindle (young cats or kittens)
Cattle: herd or drove
Colts: rag
Deer: herd
Dogs: kennel or pack
Ferrets: business
Goats: herd, tribe or trip
Greyhounds: two, a brace; three, a leash
Hares: drove, husk, trace or trip; two, a brace; three, a leash
Horses: stable or harras (stud)
Mares: stud
Mice: nest
Moles: labour
Oxen: team or drove; yolk (working oxen)
Pigs: litter
Pups: litter
Rabbits: nest
Racehorses: string or field
Sheep: flock or hurtle
Wolves: pack

FOX HUNTING

All are not hunters that blow the horn.

Fox hunting should be done handsomely.

A good hunter takes much game, not all.

Hunting can have as much pain as pleasure.

A southerly wind and a cloudy sky proclaimeth a hunting morning.

Hounds and horses devour their masters.

A hunter follows what flees.

Hunting and law are full of pitfalls.

Barking dogs are seldom good at hunting.

FOX HUNTING TERMS AND THEIR MEANINGS

At fault: When the hounds lose a scent and make a check in their running.

Billet: The excrements of a fox.

Bolt: When a fox is forced out of its earth or out of a drain.

Break: When a fox leaves the safety of a covert or wood.

Break-up: When hounds eat the carcass of a fox.

Carries a scent: This is the expression used for any land that holds the scent of a fox that has previously passed over it. Damp or moist weather helps in the retention of scent.

Cast: An effort by the huntsman to get the hounds to recover the scent of the fox after a check.

Check: When hounds temporarily lose the scent and stop running.

Chop: Hounds chop when they kill a fox while it is asleep, or when it has no chance of escape.

Course: Hounds course when they run a fox in view.

Covert: Any wood, except very large ones, that will hold a fox.

Cub: The name for a young fox up to 1 November.

Cur: Any dog other than a foxhound.

Double the horn: When the huntsman gives a succession of quick sharp notes with his horn; this is usually done when the fox has been seen by the huntsman in covert, or when the hounds speak to a find.

Draw: When the hounds, under the direction of the huntsman, move systematically through a covert.

Earth: The underground home of a fox.

Enter: When young hounds are taught to hunt.

Entered: When a hound has had a full season's cub-hunting and has shown an aptitude for hunting.

Feather: A hound 'feathers' when it is uncertain of the line of scent; it usually moves along slowly waving its stern.

Foil: Any smell which obliterates the scent of the fox. A line of scent can be foiled by other animals passing over the line taken by the fox before the hounds arrive.

Gone to ground: When the fox has returned to its earth.

Headed: When a hound or hounds have been baulked for any reason and cannot follow the scent they have picked up. This usually occurs when a fox has been turned from its course by uninitiated foot or car followers.

Heads up: When hounds have stopped feeling for the scent with their nostrils and are looking about.

Heel: When hounds have found a scent and start to run it in the opposite direction to that in which the fox was running.

Hit the line: When, after casting around, a hound picks up the scent of the fox and starts to follow it.

Lift: When the huntsman directs his hounds to a place where he knows the scent of the fox will be. This usually occurs when he or someone else has seen a fox before hounds could possibly have picked up the scent.

Line: The trail of scent left by a fox.

Mark: When hounds come to stop at an open earth or drain after following a hot scent.

Mask: A fox's head.

Mob: When hounds surround a fox so that it has no fair chance of getting away.

Music: The cry of hounds following a hot scent.

Mute: A hound is said to be mute when it does not speak or 'throw its tongue' when on the line of a fox.

Muzzle: The nose of a hound.

Own the line: This is said of a hound who confidently follows a trail of scent left by a fox.

Pad: The foot of a fox.

Point: The furthest distance that a hunted fox will take hounds, measured as the crow flies, before he is killed or escapes.

Pudding: The porridge that is usually fed to hounds.

Rate: When you have to reprove or correct a hound, you rate it.

Ride: A clear way through a wood.

Riot: This term is used when hounds leave the scent of the fox and follow that of any other animal, usually rabbit or hare.

Running: When hounds are actually on the line of a fox.

Scent: The distinctive odour of the fox. Scent can be said to be 'breast high' when hounds race on without lowering their muzzles to the ground. 'A 'burning scent' means that the fox has only recently passed over the ground.

Sinking: When the fox is slowing down at the end of a long or fast run.

Skirting: Cutting off a corner rather than following the line of scent.

Speaking: When a hound barks.

Stale line: A fox's scent which has become faint with time.

Stern: The tail of a hound.

Stopping: The closing up of the fox's earth during the night while the fox is away.

Tongue: The cry of hounds. When they are speaking to a line they are said to be throwing their tongues.

Touch the horn: When the huntsman blows the horn.

Unentered: When a hound has not finished one cub-hunting season.

View: When one sees a fox.

Vixen: A female fox.

Walk: Hound puppies are being walked when they are being

looked after by others rather than by the staff at the hunt kennels.

Whelps: Puppies that have not yet been weaned from their mothers.

Wind: A hound winds a fox when it first picks up its scent.

WORDS AND PHRASES USED WHEN SPEAKING TO HOUNDS AND OTHER HUNTING DOGS

Cope-forrard *Get away together* *Hark*	Cheers used by the whipper-in to get hounds out of covert to join those that are already on the scent and **running**.
Eloo at him, eleew	These are words of encouragement and let the hounds know that they are near to the fox and that the huntsman knows the fox is sinking.
Get-on-tweem	Lagging hounds that should be up with the huntsman are admonished with these words and, when necessary, a touch of the whip from the whipper-in.
Hark, cry hark *Huic, huic, huic* *Hark forrard to*	When one of the hounds has opened up on a scent in the covert, and it is a reliable hound that is speaking to the line, the huntsman will say these words in an urgent manner.
Leu-in	To encourage hounds to enter covert, or terriers and spaniels to enter thick cover.
Leu-try there *Leu-try in that* *Try-over, yoi-try* *Yoi-rouse 'im, yoi-wind 'im* *Hew-in and try*	When drawing a covert the huntsman will talk to his hounds using any of these phrases in an encouraging voice.

Tally O!	A cry made to draw the attention of the huntsman when a fox has been sighted going away from the covert where the hounds are still casting around.
Whoop! Wind-im there	To encourage the hounds to hold together when the fox has gone to earth and it is intended, with the help of the terrier, to dig him out.
Yo-oi, forrard on *Forra-r-r-r-rd on*	To spur hounds on to greater effort while they are actually running; addressed to hounds at the rear of the pack particularly.
Yoi-over, try back	This call is made by the huntsman at the end of a draw through covert when he wishes hounds to try on the way back because he has a strong suspicion that a fox lying-up has been missed on the draw.
Yu-bike *Lew in bike*	This is a command to hounds who have strayed out of covert while it is being drawn to get back into the wood or covert and get on with the work of finding the quarry.
Yu-tally-over-r-r	Used by the huntsman when he has seen a fox cross a ride in covert and wants to lift his hounds and bring them to the point where the fox crossed over.
Yut, yut, yut, try *Yo-hote*	The huntsman will use these words with a tone of urgency and authority when hounds have checked and he is anxious to get them back on the line.

Birds

A little bird is content with a little nest.

However high a bird may fly, it must feed near to the ground.

Every bird is known by its feathers.

It is a dirty bird that fouls its own nest.

Birds of a feather flock together.

Birds of prey do not flock together.

A bird in the hand is worth two in the bush.

The early bird catches the worm.

To scare a bird is not the way to catch it.

It is no use trying to catch old birds with chaff.

The west wind is full of birdsong.

Birds of prey do not sing.

One's lucky, two's unlucky, three's health,
Four's wealth, five's sickness, and six is death.

COCKS

A servant and a cock should be kept but one year.

Every cock can crow on his own dunghill.

If a cock goes crowing to bed, he will certainly rise with a watery
head.

If the cock moult before the hen,
We shall have weather thick and thin.
If the hen moult before the cock,
We shall have weather hard as a rock.

The winning cock can lose feathers.

CROWS

Crows bewail dead sheep and eat them.

The crow thinks her own bird fairest.

A crow is never whiter for washing.

Crows are black all the world over.

One crow does not make a winter.

Crows do not peck out other crows' eyes.

The carrion that the eagle has left will feed a crow.

No carrion will kill a crow.

If the crow would feed in silence, it would have more of a feast
and much less strife and envy.

CUCKOOS

Nightingale and cuckoo sing in one month.

He hath but one tune, like the cuckoo in June.

The cuckoo comes in April, sings his song in May,
In the middle of June he changes his tune, and then he flies
away.

The cuckoo is a purty bird, she sings as she flies,
She picks up the dirt in the spring of the year,
And sucks little birds' eggs to make her voice clear.

On April the third comes the cuckoo.

> *'Er bringeth good tidings and telleth no lies,*
> *'Er eateth sweet flowers to make her voice clear.*

When you first hear the cuckoo, turn your money.

> *When the cuckoo comes to the bare thorn,*
> *Sell your cow and buy your corn;*
> *But when she comes to the full bit,*
> *Sell your corn and buy your sheep.*

> *Heard in September,*
> *A thing to remember.*
> *Heard in October,*
> *You're not sober.*

DUCKS

Ducks lay eggs, geese lay wagers.

A duck will not lay until it has tasted Lide [March] water.

EAGLES

Eagles do not catch flies.

Eagles fly alone.

When the eagle is dead, the crow will peck out his eyes.

There is no need to teach an eagle to fly.

EGGS

Never take a stone to break an egg when a knife will do.

Send not for a hatchet to break an egg.

A black hen lays a white egg.

Eggs and oaths are easily broken.

As good an addled egg as an idle bird.

Better half an egg than an empty shell.

As full of meat as an egg.

It is very hard to shave an egg.

In the frying of eggs will be seen which one is good.

Who would have eggs must bear with the cackling.

Omelettes are not made without breaking eggs.

He that treads on eggs must tread lightly.

A wild goose never laid a tame egg.

She who cackles most lays least eggs.

Innocent as a new-laid egg.

GEESE

Before St Chad [2 March] every goose lays, both good and bad.

Feather by feather the goose is plucked.

She gabbles like a goose among swans.

Goslings lead geese to water.

It is a blind goose that knows not fox from fernbush.

A goose hisses but does not bite.

When one goose drinks, all drink.

There is not enough grass for a goose to graze.

Goose and gander and gosling are three sounds but only one thing.

The goose that goes too often to the kitchen finds a place on the spit.

He that eats the king's goose will be choked by the feathers.

If all fools wore white caps we should look like a flock of geese.

HAWKS

By hawks and hounds small profit is found.

Hold fast! The first point to learn in hawking.

Our ancestors grew not great by hawking and hunting.

Pheasants are fools who invite a hawk to dinner.

Hawks are not allured by an empty hand.

The gentle hawk half mans herself.

A carrion kite will never make a good hawk.

HENS

A whistling woman and a crowing hen,
Are good for neither God nor men.

Fat hens are ill layers.

It is a sad house where the hen crows loudest.

One chick can keep a hen busy.

A sitting hen never grows fat.

If you burn egg-shells the hens will cease to lay.

It is a bad hen that eats at home and lays away.

A neighbour's hen could well be a goose.

JAYS

Wear a jay's feather in your hat and you will never be without a penny in your pocket.

LARKS

The leg of a lark is better than the body of a kite.

He who harries a lark's nest will not thrive.

Merry larks are ploughmen's clocks.

Rise with the lark and go to bed with the lamb.

MAGPIES

One for sorrow, two for mirth,
Three for a wedding, four for a birth;
Five for silver, six for gold;
Seven for a secret not to be told;
Eight for heaven, nine for hell,
Ten for the Devil's very own sel'.

If a young woman should see a single magpie during the early morning of 15 March all hopes for a wedding in the next 12 months will be gone.

NIGHTINGALES

Nightingale and cuckoo sing in one month.

A nightingale cannot sing in a cage.

The nightingale and the cuckoo come on the third day of April.

OWLS

He is in great want of a bird that will give a groat for an owl.

An owl is not accounted wiser for living retiredly.

He that is born in a wood is not scared of an owl.

PARTRIDGES

If the partridge had the woodcock's thigh,
He would be the best bird that ever did fly.

PEACOCKS

A peacock's eyes are inclined to his tail.

When the peacock loudly bawls, there likely will be rain and squalls.

I like writing with a peacock's quill, the feathers are all eyes.

The peacock hath fine feathers, but foul feet.

PIGEONS

He shot at the pigeon and killed the crow.

RAVENS

Bring up a raven and he may peck out your eye.

A raven should not say to a rook 'stand back blackcoat'.

A raven will seek out carrion.

A raven never hatches a lark.

If a maiden should hear a raven croak while she is in bed, she should turn about left at once or she will be likely to remain a spinster for the rest of her life.

What could be rarer than a white raven?

ROBINS

He who harries a robin's nest will not survive.

> *The robin redbreast and the wren,*
> *Are God Almighty's cock and hen.*

> *Robins and wrens,*
> *Are God Almighty's friends.*
> *Martins and swallows,*
> *Are God Almighty's scholars.*

SEAGULLS

Seagull, seagull, stay on the sand,
It is never good weather when you are inland.

SPARROWS

Sparrows build in martins' nests.

A sparrow in the hand is worth more than a flying goose.

A sparrow flying behind a hawk thinks that the hawk is fleeing.

Sparrows fight for corn that is not theirs.

Sparrows should not dance with cranes, their legs are too short.

SWALLOWS

If the swallow fly high, 'tis a sign of dry.

WRENS

Wrens may prey where eagles may not perch.

He who harries a wren's nest will not thrive.

COLLECTIVE NOUNS OF BIRDS

Chickens: peep or brood
Coots: covert
Crows: murder
Curlews: herd
Doves: flight
Ducks: team (in flight); paddling (on the water)
Dunlins: flight
Eagles: convocation
Fieldfares: flock
Finches: charm
Geese: gaggle; skein (on the wing); flock (on the water)
Goldfinches: charm or trembling
Grouse: covey (single family); pack (larger gathering)
Gulls: colony
Hens: brood
Herons: siege
Jays: band
Lapwings: deceit
Larks: exaltation, flight or bevy
Magpies: tiding
Mallard: flush
Nightingales: watch
Partridges: covey (family); brace (two)
Pheasants: nye; brood (family); brace (two)
Pigeons: flock or flight
Plovers: congregation, flight, wing or stand
Pochards: rush or flight
Quail: bevy
Ravens: unkindness
Rooks: building or clamour
Snipe: walk or wisp; couple or leash (when dead)
Sparrows: host or tribe

Starlings: chattering or murmuration
Swallows: flight
Swans: herd or team
Swifts: flock
Teal: spring, coil or bunch
Thrushes: mutation
Turkeys: rafter
Widgeon: company
Woodcock: fall or flight
Woodpeckers: descent
Wrens: herd

SHOOTING

Short shooting loseth your game.

Shoot not beyond the mark.

Shooting too far never killed a bird.

Shooting often hits the mark.

Never shoot, never hit.

He who shoots most must have most hits.

He that shoots always right must forfeit his arrows.

SHOOTING TERMS

Bag: The total amount of game shot in one day.

Beaters: A line of people, whether men, women or children, with or without dogs, who advance, usually under the direction of a keeper, in a line across a covert or through woodland or moorland, striking at bushes etc. to rouse the game and make it fly in the direction of the guns.

Butt: A hide for a gun. Mainly used in grouse shooting.

Cheeper: A young game bird.

Choke: The barrel of a shotgun where the bore is narrower at one end than the other.

Drive: When game is driven by beaters towards the guns.

Drumming: This is the noise made by a snipe, usually in the breeding season, as the bird planes down in its flight.

Flankers: Men who walk at the end of a line of beaters whose job it is to stop game trying to fly out of a covert at the sides.

Flighting: A term used to describe ducks or geese coming on to water in large numbers, usually in the evenings.

Flush: To cause birds to take flight.

Gun: This term can be used to describe the sportsman if he is carrying a gun and intends to shoot with it.

Hide: A structure either natural or artificial in which a sportsman can conceal or camouflage himself.

Peg: A mark to denote the position in which a gun shall stand at any particular drive.

Planing: When a bird moves through the air without any wing movement.

Pricked: Wounded by shot but still able to fly on for a while.

Rocketing: When a bird is flying fast and high towards the gun.

Rough shooting: Usually shooting over ground that has had no special preparation in the way of rearing or preserving game artificially. It is often carried out by a person alone, with a dog or dogs to put up anything that is shootable.

Runner: A wounded or pricked bird that is still able to travel quite fast along the ground.

Sewelling: Making driven birds in a covert get up and fly rather than continue to run in front of the beaters. Usually a long cord is stretched about two feet high right across the covert and on it are tied brightly coloured flags. A man at one end of the cord keeps agitating it as the driven birds approach.

Spurs: The backward-pointing claws of a pheasant or other bird.

Strong on the wing: A term which can be applied to any bird that flies very boldly and fast.

Tower: A bird is said to tower if after being shot it soars up almost perpendicularly before it falls.

Various: This describes almost any bird or animal that is not named specifically in the game register.

Vermin: Birds of prey and wild animals that are destructive to game.

Walking up: When the guns walk in a straight line across a field, usually a field of kale or roots, with the intention of flushing any birds that may be using the crop as cover or as a feeding place.

Whirring: The sound pheasants and partridges make when they are flying.

Wild-fowling: A form of shooting almost solely concerned with water birds, either from a punt on the water or from hides, usually natural ones, in the meadows and marshlands where this type of bird may be found feeding or coming in to feed.

SNARES

The bird avoids the snare that shows.

He who fears all snares falls into none.

Fish

It is a silly fish that is caught twice on the same hook.

The best fish swim deep.

Better small fish than any empty dish.

Little fish are sweet.

Fish and guests smell at three days old.

Daughters and dead fish should never be kept.

It is no good fishing in troubled waters.

Fish are not caught with a bird call.

The fish will soon be caught that nibbles at the bait.

Winter fly-fishing is as useful as an out-of-date almanac.

Young fish and old flesh are best.

Never a fisherman would there be if fish could hear as well as see.

A hook is well lost in catching a salmon.

Take a drink when eating fish.

> *When the wind is in the east, then the fishes do bite the least;*
> *When the wind is in the west, then the fishes do bite the best;*
> *When the wind is in the north, then the fishes do come forth;*
> *When the wind is in the south, it blows the bait into the fish's*
> *mouth.*

All fish they get that cometh to the net.

COLLECTIVE NOUNS OF FISH

Catch: The number of fish caught at any one time.
Cran: A measure of fresh herrings – 37½ gallons (about 750 fish).
Draught: The take of fish in one drawing of the net.
Flote: A shoal.
Flutter of jellyfish.
Haul: The draught of a fishing-net.
Run: A shoal of fish in motion, especially ascending a river from the sea for spawning.
School: A shoal or large number of fish, porpoises, whales etc. swimming together whilst feeding or migrating.
Shoal: A school.
Shot: The throw and haul-in of a fishing-net.

SOME FISHING TERMS AND NAMES

Adipose fin: A dorsal fin on members of the salmon family, set near the tail.

Alderman: An old name for a chub.

Alevin: A newly-hatched trout or salmon after it has emerged from the ovum and has the yolk sac still attached.

Anal fin: A fin on the underside of a fish near the tail.

Backing: A fine but strong line, fastened to the dressed line and attached to the reel drum: It acts as a reserve when a fish has taken an unusually long run. It also serves to fill the reel to a proper level to allow line to be wound in more rapidly.

Baggit: A female salmon after spawning.

Banker: A trout lying close to the bank.

Birds' nest: A line which is tangled, usually because of an over-run while casting a spinner.

Bob fly: The top fly of a cast of three or more wet flies.

Brace: Two fish of the same kind.

Brandling: A red worm used as bait.

Cannibal: A fish that will prey on its own species.

Cast: A short length, usually about three yards, of transparent nylon or gut attached to the line at one end and the fly at the other. (Today, the word 'leader' is more often used). Also, the act of throwing the fly or bait.

Caudal fin: The tail of a fish.

Chuck and chance it: To cast flies without knowing where a fish may be lying, or when no rise has been seen. Sometimes the term is applied to wet fly-fishing generally.

Coarse fish: Any fish other than 'game' fish; that is, other than salmon, trout, or sea trout.

Cock fish: A male fish.

Cocking a fly: Casting in such a manner that the fly sits high upon the water.

Collar: A length of gut attached to the line, for joining to the cast.

Coming short: When a fish is not taking the fly properly.

Covering a fish: When the fisherman gets his fly over the place where the fish is lying or rising.

Creel: A basket for carrying the fish that have been caught.

Devon minnow: An artificial spinning bait shaped like a minnow, with hooks attached.

Disgorger: An instrument for removing hooks from fish after they have been caught.

Dressed line: A line that has been made waterproof, or treated to ensure that it floats.

Dropper: A fly tied to a short piece of gut fixed at right angles to the cast above the tail fly.

Drowned: A fly or line that has become waterlogged and will no longer float.

Dun: A name for various artificial flies, often dark coloured, made to resemble a natural fly in its early winged state.

Educated trout: One that seems well aware of the artifices of the fisherman.

Elver: A young eel. Elvers are caught in their thousands as they make their way up rivers in the spring.

Fine: This term describes tackle when it is thin or light.

Finnock: Young sea trout in its grilse state. A Scots term.

Flight of hooks: Two or more triangles.

Float: Usually made with some light material, like cork, which is buoyant. It has two main uses: it keeps the bait off the bottom and it indicates, when it sinks or quivers, that a fish is biting or has taken the bait.

Fork tail: A grilse.

Foul hooked: When a fish is hooked in any part of its body other than its mouth.

Fresh run: A migratory fish, salmon or sea trout, that has recently come from the sea and is now in fresh water.

Fry: Recently hatched young fish, between the alevin and yearling stages.

Gaff: A large hook fixed to a handle used for taking big fish from the water after they have been played out.

Gentles: Maggots; used for bait.

Gills: The part of a fish through which it breathes.

Grilse: A young salmon returning from the sea during the first year of migration.

Hackle: A neck feather of a bird, used in making artificial flies, usually to represent legs and antennae.

Handling: Bringing a fish in by pulling the line rather than using the reel.

Harling: When a fly or other bait is trailed behind a boat.

Hatchery: A fish farm.

Head and tail rise: This describes the manner in which some fish break the surface of the water when feeding – first with their head and then with their tail.

Hen fish: A female fish.

Jack: A small pike.

Jigging: When a salmon, after being hooked, shakes its head to get rid of the fly or bait.

Kelt: A salmon that has recently spawned and is returning to the sea. In this condition salmon are unfit for food, and their capture is illegal.

Ladder: A man-made series of steps and pools to assist salmon to negotiate difficult or unjumpable weirs and waterfalls.

Landing net: A net on a handle, used by the fisherman to lift out of the water the fish that he has been playing. The cast would break if used on its own.

Lave net: Like a very large shrimping net, used for taking salmon by a man wading.

Leader: See *Cast*.

Leash: Three fish of the same kind.

Ledgering: Fishing on the bottom of a river or pool. The line is passed through a lead weight which rests on the bottom.

Lies: Places where salmon stop for a while on their way upstream.

Limit: The number of fish that may be caught on any one occasion, or the size of fish that may be retained.

Live-baiting: Fishing with a live fish as bait.

Maiden: A fish that has never spawned.

Milt: Fish semen.

Mount a cast: To tie flies on to the cast preparatory to wet fly-fishing.

Neb: The nose, usually of a cock fish.

Nymph: The first, underwater, stage of a fly subsequent to leaving the egg.

Old soldier: A male salmon after spawning.

Otter: A line with many flies on it and attached to a board; used in poaching.

Ova: Fish eggs.

Parr: Salmon or sea trout fry, which lives in fresh water for the early part of its life before going to sea.

Paste: A mixture made of flour, bread or other ingredients and water, for use as bait in coarse fishing.

Paternostering: A form of bottom fishing, with hooks suspended away from the line by booms.

Playing: Allowing the fish to take out line and then reeling in. A process repeated to tire a lively fish before it is landed.

Plummet: A weight attached to a line and used to measure the depth of the water.

Pricked: A fish that has felt the hook but has got away.

Priest: A weighted instrument used for killing fish.

Pumping: Lifting and lowering the rod when playing a difficult fish in deep water in order to bring it to land without putting too much strain on the rod.

Putchers: A special type of basket trap used on the Severn.

Putting down: When fish are frightened and move away so that they will not look at a fly.

Redds: Spawning beds.

Reel in: To wind in the line.

Ripe fish: Fish that are ready to spawn.

Rise: Rings on the water showing that fish are coming to the surface to feed.

Roe: The ova of fish.

Run: A run is the fast part of a river. To run is to take out a line once a fish is hooked.

Running salmon: Salmon that are moving constantly up-river.

Sea lice: Sea insects clinging to the bodies of migratory fish after they have entered fresh water.

Sewin: Sea trout; a word used in Wales.

Shooting the line: While casting a fly, allowing a quantity of line held in the hand to run out through the rings on the rod.

Shot: Split metal shot pinched on to the cast to sink the bait and cock the float.

Smoking: Water is said to be smoking when mist is rising from it.

Smolt: Young salmon or sea trout going to the sea for the first time.

Spey cast: A cast which does not involve bringing the line and fly behind the angler. Used to avoid catching obstacles, for example trees or rocks.

Spinning: Fishing with a revolving bait.

Spoon: A spinning bait shaped like the bowl of a spoon.

Springer: A salmon entering the river in the early spring.

Square tail: Sea trout.

Stale fish: A migratory fish, salmon or sea trout, that has been in the river for a long time.

Stand: A convenient, usual or prepared place from which to fish.

Stew pond: A fish pond.

Strike: To raise the point of your rod when the fish is mouthing your bait or fly, so that the hook becomes fixed in its mouth.

Strip a fish: To gently squeeze out the ova or milt. A word used in hatching operations.

Stripping line: Pulling line off the reel.

Swim: A part of the river, usually deep and steady, where fish are lying in wait for food coming down to them.

Swivel: This is fastened to the top of a spinning bait to prevent the line twisting; it is essential when spinning.

Tackle: Fishing gear.

Tag: The tail end of an artificial fly.

Tail fly: When more than one fly is being used, the tail fly is the one tied to the end of the cast.

Tailer: A wire loop used for landing salmon.

Tickling: Putting your hands carefully in the water behind an unsuspecting trout, tickling under its belly, and suddenly throwing it out of the water. A method used by poachers.

Travelling: When a migratory fish is moving upstream.

Troll: To trail a bait or fly behind a boat.

Tying flies: Making artificial flies.

Umber: An old name for the grayling.

Wagtail: A form of spinning bait.

Weeded: When a hooked fish has taken refuge in the weeds. There is a danger then of the cast getting tangled and breaking.

Whipping the water: Casting unskilfully.

Whitling: Young sea trout.

Wiggler: An artificial bait which wobbles.

Working the fly: Keeping an artificial fly moving through the water.

Yellow fin: An immature seatrout; one of several popular names.
Yolk sac: An umbilical food sac carried by the alevin when it
emerges from the ovum.

Insects

ANTS

An ant hath wings to her own hurt.

What would an ant do if it had the head of a bull?

Go to the ant thou sluggard, consider her ways and be wise.

Be like the ant in the days of summer.

BEES

A swarm of bees cannot be turned.

A dead bee makes no honey.

Bees have honey in their mouths, but stings in their tails.

When bees are old they yield no honey.

A swarm of bees in May is worth a load of hay.
A swarm of bees in June is worth a silver spoon.
A swarm of bees in July isn't worth a fly.

FLIES

Who would not lose a fly to catch a trout?

Flies haunt lean horses.

The fly that plays in the candle must surely singe his wings.

Flies come not to a boiling pot.

Hungry flies bite sore.

Flies come to feasts unasked.

PART FIVE

Nature at Work

Herbs and Wild Flowers
Their Uses in Healing

The ancient uses of herbs and wild flowers as cures are given here for interest's sake only. Their application, particularly internally, is highly inadvisable without expert advice.

AGRIMONY

Used to cure *snake bites*.

A tea made of agrimony flowers with lemon added was used to cure *colds*.

Agrimony was originally used for the *flavouring of beer*.

ALECOST (COSTMARY)

For *bee stings* rub the affected part with the bruised leaves.

The roots were formerly used to *flavour ale*.

ANGELICA

A *general tonic* taken as tea, but do not drink too much.

Leaves can be used as a *poultice*.

It was believed that if a sprig of angelica was held in the mouth it would be a safeguard against *infectious diseases*.

Eaten raw small quantities are an aid to *digestion*.

A decoction will relieve *flatulence*, but do not take too much.

If a small amount of angelica is added to *rhubarb* while the rhubarb is cooking it will help to remove *excess tartness*.

ARCHANGEL, WHITE (WHITE DEAD NETTLE)

Take tea sweetened with honey for *chills*.

ARNICA

Rub *sprains* and *bruises* with the flowers.

Used for *chilblains*.

BASIL

Can be taken for *nervous disorders* as a decoction or as snuff made from the crushed dried leaves. The snuff is also useful for *clearing the head*.

The presence of basil in the garden is a safeguard against *witchcraft*.

Basil will help to dispel *flies*.

BAY

A tea made from bay will stimulate the *appetite*.

BEARBERRY

A decoction made with the crushed leaves will relieve *kidney troubles*.

BELLADONNA (DEADLY NIGHTSHADE)

Can be used in liniments, lotions and plasters for the relief of *rheumatism*. All parts of the plant can be fairly poisonous to both man and animals if eaten.

BERGAMOT

The tea acts as a *tonic*.

Red bergamot tea taken while it is hot will help *relaxation* and *induce sleep*.

BETONY

The dried and powdered leaves can be made into a nostrum for the cure of *headaches*.

A protection against *witches* and *evil spirits*.

BLACK HOREHOUND

Recommended as a cure for the *bite of a mad dog*, and to stop *convulsions*.

BORAGE

Can be added to drinks to provide an extra *stimulant*.

A decoction will help to reduce *fever*.

CALAMINT

An infusion of 1 oz. dried leaves to 1 pint boiling water will relieve *flatulence*.

CAMOMILE

Note: Use with caution, too much camomile can be harmful.

A tea made from the flowers and taken hot will aid *digestion* and be good for *stomach upsets*.

When cold it can be used for *bathing the eyes*, as a *hair rinse*, and as a *mouth wash*.

As a cold tea it is *soothing to the skin* and has been known to cure *eczema*.

An infusion of 1 oz. dried flowers to 1 pint boiling water will act as a *sedative*.

The flowers can be used in a bag as a poultice to help reduce all *swellings*.

CARAWAY

An essential ingredient for *love potions*.

CHERVIL

This herb was used in food extensively during Lent as it was thought to *purify the blood* and *cleanse the whole body*.

CHICKWEED

Good for *obesity*.

Good for *boils*, *abscesses* and *carbuncles*, for which the leaves are boiled and pressed to make a *poultice*.

Bathe *sore eyes* with cold tea made from chickweed.

CHICORY

A decoction made from 1 oz. of the root to 1 pint water will be effective for *jaundice, gout* and *rheumatism.*

CHIVES

When eaten raw in salads, chives will stimulate the *appetite,* be good for the *kidneys* and help to reduce *blood pressure.*

CINQUEFOIL

The outer bark of the root, taken up in April and dried, and then made into a decoction by boiling 2 oz. of the root in 1 quart of water until the liquid is reduced to 1 pint, is a remedy for *diarrhoea.*

The dried leafy tops can be steeped in water for 15 minutes and the liquid taken three times a day, and this is also effective for *diarrhoea.*

CLOVER

Tea made from 1 oz. flowers and leaves to 1 pint water is good for *kidneys, catarrh, nerves* and *flatulence.* Drink a wineglassful, undiluted, several times a day. The infusions may be sweetened with honey or made more palatable with a squeeze of lemon.

COLTSFOOT

Note: Do *not* eat.

Inhale the smoke from the dried leaves to cure a *cough* and to relieve *asthma.*

COMFREY

Use the leaves to heal *cuts* and *wounds.*

Use the roots for *poultices.*

Tea made from comfrey is good for *chest complaints.*

Make a decoction from 1 oz. of the crushed root, a wineglassful to be taken three times a day, for the cure of *diarrhoea* and *dysentery.*

COMMON BUCKTHORN

A very *strong purgative* can be made from the bark. *Note*: The berries are dangerous to children when eaten.

COUCHGRASS

Take tea made from the washed roots for *rheumatism, gout, kidneys* and *bladder.*

DAISY

Tea made from the flowers and leaves – 1 oz. to 1 pint water – is good for *varicose veins.*

DANDELION

Take tea for clearing the skin of *eczema.*

Tea can be used as a slight *purgative,* and to relieve *sore eyes.*

Eat the leaves in a salad for a good *complexion,* to stimulate the *liver* or to relieve *gall bladder trouble.*

DILL

A decoction made from the seeds makes a soothing mixture for the relief of *colic, flatulence* and *hiccoughs.*

DOG ROSE

The ripe hips are an excellent source of *Vitamin B* if made into jam or jelly. Take care with the hairy coating of the seeds inside as they can be a very unpleasant irritant.

ELDER

Note: The raw seeds are emetically poisonous.

The bruised leaves can be used to deter *flies*.

Take mulled elderflower wine to cure *colds*.

Take ground elder tea for *gout* and *kidney flushing*. Used externally, the tea is good for *rheumatism*.

A strong infusion made from the dried blossom and flavoured with mint and sweetened with honey is a cure for *influenza*.

To make elderflower water pack the flowers only into a large jug or other container and pour $\frac{1}{2}$ gallon boiling water over them. Cover with a cloth and leave to stand for 24 hours. Strain and use internally for *stomach upsets* and *headaches*, and externally for clear *skin* and for warding off *biting insects*.

Elderflower cream (see p. 168) is good for the *complexion*.

EUCALYPTUS

Bruise the leaves and inhale the fumes to relieve and cure *colds*.

FENNEL

Use a decoction to bathe *sore eyes*.

Eat any part of the plant to *reduce weight*.

Take tea made from ½ pint boiling water poured on to 1 teaspoonful seeds for a *mild laxative* and to soothe *stomach pains*.

Fennel was much used in the past during Lent as it was supposed to *satisfy hunger* during the periods of fasting.

A compress soaked in cold fennel tea is *soothing for the eyes*, and if mixed with honey will help to *dispel wrinkles*.

FLAX (LINSEED)

Make a *poultice* with the seeds to *reduce inflammation*.

An infusion of 1 teaspoonful seed to 1 pint boiling water, left until it is well steeped, is a cure for *coughs* and *colds*.

GARLIC

Will help to *reduce blood pressure*.

Garlic is a valuable *antiseptic* and can be used as a deterrent to *infection*.

Take garlic to assist in promoting *perspiration*.

GOOD KING HENRY

The leaves were used extensively in the past as *cabbage*, but the introduction of spinach put an end to its use for this purpose.

The leaves can be used as a *poultice*.

The roots can be fed to *sheep* to cure *coughs*.

The ground seeds make a *substitute flour* for bread.

GREAT BURDOCK

The roots or leaves, if well pounded and boiled in goose-grease, make an excellent *ointment* for all *skin complaints*.

GROUND IVY

Note: The berries are poisonous to children.

Used to make *beer* before the introduction of hops.

An infusion of a good handful of the leaves with 1 pint boiling water can be taken as a *tonic* to *purify the blood*.

An infusion of leaves can also be used as a fomentation for *bruises* and for the *removal of shiny patches on clothes*.

HEDGE WOUNDWORT

This plant was considered to have great *healing qualities* and was regularly used to make *poultices* and *ointment*.

HERB BENNET (HEMLOCK)

Note: May be fatal if eaten.

It was once thought that if this plant grew near a house it had the *power to protect* the house against the *Devil*.

The roots have a very *pleasant smell*, rather like clover.

HERB ROBERT

When the flowers hang downwards it is a sign of *impending bad weather*.

HORSERADISH

Horseradish is an *antiseptic* and aids *digestion* after a rich meal.

A cure for *flatulence*: take 2 oz. scraped horseradish, ½ oz. mustard seed and a pinch of salt. Cover with boiling vinegar. Leave to steep for 24 hours, strain and bottle. When needed, mix 1 teaspoonful in a glassful of hot water and sip slowly.

HORSETAIL

Note: Use in *small* quantities.

Make a decoction from the washed roots for all *bladder disorders*.

An astringent decoction made from the roots of horsetail should be used regularly to *tighten up the tissues*.

The roots contain silicic acid and can be used to clean *copper, brass* and *pewter*.

HYSSOP

Make an infusion from dried flowers for *chest complaints* and for *catarrh*.

An infusion of hyssop and white horehound in equal parts is good for *rheumatism*.

JUNIPER

Tea made from the berries is considered a good *general purpose medicine* as it will stimulate the *appetite*, cleanse the *blood*, dissolve *mucus*, improve the function of *kidneys* and relieve *gout* and *rheumatism*. The tea is made by crushing 12 to 18 berries, according to the size of cup to be used, and boiling them in slightly more than a cupful of water for about fifteen minutes.

LADY'S MANTLE

Apply direct to heal *wounds* and *sores*.

An infusion of either fresh or dried leaves taken four times a day in a wineglass is a cure for *jaundice* and other *liver troubles*.

The dried leaves made into a pillow will *induce sleep*.

LEMON BALM

The tea will help to dispel *fatigue* and makes a very *refreshing drink*.

Use in flavouring *salads* and *cider cup*.

LOVAGE

An infusion made from the dried leaves makes a *pleasant, cooling drink*.

LUNGWORT (JERUSALEM COWSLIP)

Take an infusion of 1 teaspoonful dried leaves to 1 cupful boiling water three times a day for *whooping cough*.

MARIGOLD

Apply the leaves direct for *inflammation* and *cuts*.

A decoction made from the flowers is good for the *heart* and *blood circulation*.

MARJORAM

An excellent *disinfectant*, and can be used as a *throat gargle* and *mouthwash*.

Take an infusion of a handful of fresh tops to 1 pint water for *headaches*.

The dried leaves can be heated and applied direct to act as a *fomentation* or *poultice*.

MEADOWSWEET

Take an infusion of 1 oz. dried flowers to 1 pint boiling water to cure a *cold*.

Steep the fresh flowers of meadowsweet in rain water for 24 hours and then boil the liquid for 5 minutes and take for *fever* and *colic*.

MELILOT

This plant was introduced into Britain for the sole purpose of using it in the making of *poultices*.

MOTHERWORT

A tea made from the leaves and flowers can be used as a *nerve tonic* and as a *stimulant* for the *heart*.

MUGWORT

Mugwort tea has been found to be of value to *diabetics*. It will also relieve *rheumatic pains*.

NETTLE

Infuse a handful of leaves with 1 pint boiling water and take for *rheumatism*.

For *severe cases of rheumatism* whip the affected part of the patient with old nettles.

Nettle tea should be taken regularly as a *tonic*. Young shoots gathered in the spring and dried are just as effective for making the tea as fresh leaves.

Stinging nettle tea is good for *sore throats, bronchitis, asthma* and *rheumatism*. Make the tea with a small quantity of tops – three or four – to 1 pint water. Take a wineglassful twice daily.

Young nettle tops can be used as a *vegetable*.

PARSLEY

A decoction of parsley will help to *remove freckles* and *moles*.

Parsley tea alleviates *kidney disorders*. It is also a *source of iron*.

PERIWINKLE

Note: This plant is poisonous if eaten.

To cure *cramp* tie bands of periwinkle round the affected part.

An ointment made from the bruised leaves and lard without salt is good for *inflammation of the skin*.

Place bruised leaves in the nose to stop *nose bleeds*.

PURGING FLAX

This is an excellent *laxative* when taken as a tea.

RAMPION

The fleshy roots of this plant were often used in *salads*.

ROCK SAMPHIRE or ST PETER'S HERB

The thick fleshy parts of the leaf can be made into *pickles*.

ROSEMARY

To cure *gout* apply the bruised leaves and stems to the affected part.

An infusion of the dried leaves and flowers mixed with a little borax is a *tonic for hair*.

Take tea made of 1 oz. flowers and tops to 1 pint water for *headaches*.

Tea will also *stimulate blood circulation*.

The leaves can be used as an effective *moth repellent*.

When the stalks are burnt they will act as an *air freshener* in a sickroom.

Where rosemary flourishes, the lady rules.

RUE

Take tea made from rue for *flatulence*, *coughs* and *croup*, but not too much as it could make you ill.

SAGE

Drink tea made from sage – a handful of leaves to 1 pint water – for *indigestion, liver complaints* and *colds*.

Rub teeth with sage after meals to *deter tooth decay*.

Burn the dried tops of sage to *dispel infectious diseases*.

A tea made from *red sage* (purple leaved) used as a *gargle* will help to cure a *sore throat*.

He that would live for aye must eat sage in May.

A sage bush will thrive or decline as the master's business prospers or declines.

ST JOHN'S WORT

If you carry a bunch of St John's wort you will be *protected* against *witchcraft*.

SALAD BURNET

This plant has a flavour of cucumber and was regularly used in *salads* and *sauces*.

SCARLET PIMPERNEL
or POOR MAN'S WEATHER GLASS

Country men set great store by this plant as a *guide to the weather* during harvesting. If the flowers were open in the morning it would be a fine day; if they failed to open you could be sure that it would rain or turn stormy before the day was out.

SELF HEAL

An infusion of 1 oz. self heal to 1 pint water sweetened with honey and taken in a wineglass every 2 hours is good for *sore throats*.

Tea made from self heal taken regularly will ensure *good health*.

SILVERWEED

Take tea made from silverweed to relieve *ulcers* and *gallstones*, and to promote a *clear skin*.

Silverweed was used extensively to relieve *sores* and *ulcers* by applying the plant directly. It was also used to *relieve tired feet* by placing the leaves in the boots.

When food was short the roots of silverweed were ground into a mealy *flour* and made into *bread* or *cake*. The roots were also *eaten raw* or *cooked*.

SORREL

Make an infusion from a handful of sorrel to 1 pint water and drink cold to *relieve fever*.

SOUTHERNWOOD

1 teaspoonful of the dried and powdered plant in 1 teaspoonful of treacle will cure children who have *worms*.

SUMMER SAVORY

To relieve *bee* or *wasp stings* rub a bruised leaf on the affected part.

SWEET CICELY (MYRRH)

An infusion will relieve *coughs* and *flatulence*.

Boil the roots and eat with olive oil and vinegar to promote *strength* and *courage*.

TANSY

An infusion of a handful of tansy to 1 pint water taken night and morning in a teacup on an empty stomach will get rid of *worms*. It is also a stimulant for the *kidneys*. *Note*: Human poisoning has occurred from overdoses of the oil, or infusions, of tansy which has been taken medicinally.

To relieve *gout* and *rheumatism* apply the bruised leaves and stems of tansy in the form of a poultice to the affected part. Change the dressing frequently.

THYME

Use an infusion as a *mouthwash* and *gargle*.

Thyme can be used as an *antiseptic* both internally and externally.

Taken with or after eating rich food thyme will *stimulate the appetite* and *help the digestion*.

VALERIAN

Note: Use with caution, too much can be dangerous.

A powerful *stimulant* for the *nerves*.

It will cause *noises in the head* to cease.

A tea made from the dried roots acts as a strong *sedative*.

VERBENA

Tea made from verbena will cure *insomnia* and *persistent headaches*.

A decoction is good for *stomach aches* and *indigestion*.

WATERCRESS

Eat watercress for a *clear complexion*.

Rub the skin with bruised leaves to help remove *blemishes* and *spots*.

WHITE HOREHOUND

A decoction is good for *sore throats, coughs, bronchitis* and *indigestion*.

An infusion – 1 oz. to 1 pint water – will help cure the *common cold*.

White horehound is used in the making of *beer*.

To relieve a very stubborn *cough*, boil a double handful of leaves in 1 quart water for 20 minutes. Press out all the juice and strain, add lemon and honey to taste, and take a wineglassful every 2 hours.

WILLOW HERB

Tea made from the roots and leaves is good for *whooping cough* and *hiccoughs*.

WOODRUFF

Use fresh leaves as a poultice to *heal wounds*.

If used as a *flavouring for drinks*, particularly cider or pure apple juice, woodruff will help to *relax tension* and *relieve headaches*.

WOOD SAGE

A tea made from wood sage (this is the wild flower, not the cultivated herb) used to be known as a cure for *rheumatism*.

WORMWOOD

Tea made from 1 oz. leaves to 1 pint water will prevent *seasickness*.

Gather dry leaves in the late summer and make a decoction to cure *worms* and reduce *fever*.

Wormwood will keep away *moths* and *insects*.

YARROW

Rub yarrow on to a *wound* to stop it *bleeding*.

Tea made from yarrow promotes perspiration to help with *fevers* and *colds*, also *kidney disorders* and *jaundice*. Make the tea with 1 oz. dried leaves to 1 pint water. Drink it warm, 2 wineglassfuls a day.

YELLOW BEDSTRAW

As the name implies, this plant was used extensively, after it had been dried, to *stuff mattresses*, as it was very sweet-smelling and could easily be replaced when it became soiled. The plant had two other uses: the flowers were used for *curdling milk* for the making of *cheese*, and a *red dye* was extracted from the stems.

Cures

These cures are given for interest's sake only. Their application, particularly internally, is highly inadvisable without expert advice.

A doubtful remedy is better than none.

Devils must be driven out by devils.

Different sores must have different salves.

It is easy to hurt but hard to cure.

Oblivion is the best remedy for injury.

Patience is a remedy for all suffering.

Physicians cure, but nature heals.

Take care that the remedy does not exceed the ill.

Where there is right, there is remedy.

What doth it avail to pluck but one thorn out of many?

There is a remedy for all things except death.

> *Eat leeks in March and wild garlic in May,*
> *And all the year the doctors may play.*

Hang an onion up in the house and maladies will be drawn to it instead of to the occupants of the house.

If children are passed through the branches of a growing maple tree they will be assured of a long life.

GENERAL TONICS

There are a number of herbs that are recommended for making tea that has a tonic value. Most of these herbs are known to have a high mineral and trace element content. They are as follows: *agrimony, balm, bergamot, lovage,* and *sweet cicely (myrrh).* All these teas are made from a handful of the leaves to 1 pint boiling water. Keep the container covered while the infusion is taking place.

Another tonic can be made by taking a handful of *raspberry leaves* and one *blackcurrant leaf* and infusing as for ordinary tea, by pouring boiling water on to them. Sweeten to taste.

ABSCESSES

Make a poultice with *chickweed* and place it on the affected part.

ACNE

Steep 24 *daisies* in 1½ pints boiling water, and then leave to strain. Use the liquid as a lotion every night at bedtime.

AGUE

Pour 1 pint boiling water on to some *ash bark* until it is covered. Let it infuse. A wineglassful of the tea should be taken three times a day.

ASTHMA

Linseed tea: pour ½ pint boiling water on to ½ oz. linseed and let it infuse for ½ hour. Strain and sweeten with *honey. Orange or lemon* flavour may be added, but it is best taken in its natural state. It is a soothing drink and will alleviate many internal sufferings, especially asthma.

Tea made from *stinging nettles* taken three times a day will also provide relief.

BITES (INSECTS)

To deter insects from biting, make a decoction from *elder leaves* and when cool rub on to the exposed parts of the body. *Note*: Take care not to consume the raw seeds; they are emetically poisonous.

BLACK EYES

Crush the root of *Solomon's seal* and make a poultice. *Note*: *Solomon's seal* is poisonous if eaten.

BLADDER

Make a decoction of the washed roots of *horsetail* for all bladder disorders.

BLEEDING

To stop bleeding take ripe *puffballs*, break warily, sprinkle the powder on the wounds and bind. *Note*: Most *puffballs* are edible when young but not when ripe.

BLOOD

To purify the blood take regular doses of *brimstone* mixed with *treacle* or *sarsaparilla*.

A decoction made from the *flowers of marigold* will help to promote good circulation.

BOILS

Find a *bramble shoot* that has grown out of the hedge in the shape of a loop, the top having taken root in the ground, and pass your body underneath. This is also recommended as a cure for many children's ailments, having the same curative effects as passing a child through the *split* in the *trunk* of a *tree* has for measles and whooping cough.

Make pills the size of a pea from *cobbler's heel-ball* and swallow three a day.

Take a few leaves of *sage*, boil them in 1 pint *milk*, and drink this quantity once a day for nine days.

For boils and growths apply an ointment made from *foxglove* leaves and *unsalted lard* or *goose-grease*. *Note*: All parts of the foxglove can be fatally poisonous if eaten.

BOWELS

Ash leaves steeped in water for 24 hours will purge the bowels of all stoppages.

Steep the *bark* of the *buckthorn* in water for 24 hours. Drink a wineglassful of the liquid three times a day until the bowels are working naturally. *Note*: The berries are poisonous to children.

Make an infusion of *elder bark* and take a wineglassful three times a day until the bowels are cleared. *Note*: Raw *elder seeds* are emetically poisonous.

Boil 1 oz. *dandelion root* in 1½ pints water for 15 minutes. Strain carefully and take half a cupful three times a day for a mild aperient.

Tea made from *lime flowers* will soothe pain in the bowels. Pain can also be relieved with an infusion of *willow bark*.

Tea made from ½ pint boiling water poured on to 1 teaspoonful *fennel seeds* will make a good mild laxative to soothe stomach pains.

Dandelion tea makes a mild purgative that is safe for children.

BRONCHITIS

Hyssop tea: Take ¼ oz. *dried hyssop flowers* and infuse these in 1 pint boiling water for 15 minutes; sweeten with *honey*. Take a wineglassful three times a day.

Stinging nettle tea will relieve bronchitis.

Violet tea: 1 heaped teaspoonful *dried violet flowers* to ½ pint boiling water. Infuse for 5 minutes, sweeten with *honey*. This makes a soothing drink for all who suffer from bronchitis and catarrh.

BRUISES

Rub the affected part with the *flowers of arnica*, or with the *crushed root of Solomon's seal. Note*: *Solomon's seal* is poisonous when eaten.

BURNS

Bruise an *onion* and a *potato* in a mortar; add 1 tablespoonful *olive oil*, apply this pulp to the naked burn or scald, and secure it with a bandage.

Crush *dried oak-apples*, make into a paste and apply directly to the affected part.

CARBUNCLES

Apply hot poultices made from *chickweed* to the affected part until the carbuncle comes to a head and bursts.

CATARACTS (IN SHEEP)

Crush an *ivy leaf*, and when well broken down mix with *saliva* and put on the affected eye. *Note*: *Ground ivy berries* are poisonous to children.

CATARRH

Drink a wineglassful of *hyssop tea* (see above, under BRONCHITIS) three times a day for the relief of catarrh.

Clover tea made from the leaves and flowers will also relieve catarrh.

CHEST COMPLAINTS

An infusion made from the *dried flowers of hyssop* will relieve pains in the chest.

CHILBLAINS

Take the *pulp* of a *baked turnip* and mix with it 1 tablespoonful each of *olive oil, mustard* and *grated horseradish.* Rub into the affected parts and cover.

Apply a poultice of *boiled turnips*, and afterwards a poultice of *boiled groundsel* to get rid of chilblains. *Note*: *Groundsel* is poisonous when eaten.

Put 1½ oz. *olive oil*, 1 oz. *spermaceti*, 1 oz. *virgin wax*, 1 oz. *camphor*, and 2 oz. *honey* in a covered basin and place the covered basin in a pan containing a little hot water by the fire or in an open oven, where it should remain until all the ingredients are dissolved. Stir well together until it is quite cold and then apply to chilblains.

CHILLS

Drink a tea made from the *white dead nettle* sweetened with *honey* for chills.

COLDS

Drink *mulled elderberry wine* to cure a cold.

Inhale the *scent* of bruised *eucalyptus leaves* to relieve a cold in the head.

An infusion made from 1 teaspoonful *linseed* and 1 pint boiling water which has been left to steep for 12 hours is a certain cure for a cold.

To cure the common cold, take an infusion made from *white horehound,* or an infusion of 1 oz. *dried meadowsweet flowers* to 1 pint boiling water, taken three times a day.

Make a tea of 1 oz. *dried yarrow* to 1 pint boiling water. Drink warm, 2 wineglassfuls a day.

Take a handful of *elder flowers* and one of *peppermint,* place in a jug and pour 1½ pints boiling water over it. Let it steep for 30 minutes on the hob. Strain and sweeten with *honey or black treacle.* Drink hot in bed. The more you drink the sooner you will be cured. *Note:* Raw *elder seeds* are emetically poisonous.

Boil a *sprig of rosemary* in ½ pint cider for 15 minutes and drink it at bedtime as hot as possible. It will cause a great deal of perspiration, so get into bed as soon as possible.

Take thirty drops of *sal volatile, camphorated* if possible, in a small wineglassful of warm water five or six times a day.

Drink tea made from *sage* – a handful of leaves to 1 pint water – to cure a cold.

COLIC

A decoction made from the *seeds of dill* will make a soothing mixture for the relief of colic.

Steep the *fresh flowers of meadowsweet* in rain water for 24 hours and then boil the liquid for 5 minutes. Drink the liquid to help cure a colic.

COMPLEXION

To maintain a clear complexion eat *watercress* regularly. *Dandelion leaves* will have a similar effect.

Buttercup ointment: Put ½ lb. *pure vaseline* in a pan and melt. Then add as many *buttercup flowers* (not stems) as the liquid will cover. Simmer for ¾ hour, strain and pot. The ointment is ready for use as soon as it is cold, and it is good for all kinds of skin disorders. *Note:* *Buttercups* are poisonous if they are taken internally.

Cucumber lotion: Reduce 4 *large cucumbers* to pulp by steaming and passing through a fine sieve. Dissolve a good pinch of *borax* in *distilled rosewater* (½ pint to 4 oz. pulp), slowly add 30 drops *simple tincture of benzoin*, stirring briskly. Add the rosewater to the pulp, thoroughly mix, and then bottle. Apply to the face night and morning.

Elderflower cream: Melt ½ lb. *pure vaseline* and add as many *elderflowers* stripped from the stalk as the melted vaseline will cover, then simmer gently, do not boil, for at least 1 hour. Strain through muslin, add a few drops of *lavender oil*, and screw down in small jars. Note: Raw *elder seeds* are emetically poisonous.

Wash your face in dew on the first day of May and you will have a good complexion, which should help you find a husband.

CORNS

Cut corns when the *moon* is on the *wane* and *soak the feet* in warm water. Crush some *ivy leaves*, pound well and use as a plaster. Renew the leaves daily and in fifteen days the corn should drop out. *Note*: *Ground ivy berries* are poisonous to children if eaten.

COUGHS

Linseed tea made from 1 oz. seed to 1 pint boiling water will bring relief.

For a stubborn cough, boil a double handful of *white horehound leaves* in 1 quart water for 20 minutes. Press out all the juice and strain. Add *lemon* and *honey* to taste and take a wineglassful every 2 hours.

Rue tea will relieve a tickling cough, but do not take too much as it could make you ill.

An infusion of *sweet cicely* (*myrrh*) taken as required will relieve a cough.

Mix thoroughly equal parts of *honey* and *white vinegar* and take 1 teaspoonful whenever the cough is troublesome.

Inhale the smoke from the *dried leaves* of *coltsfoot* to cure a cough. *Note*: Do not eat *coltsfoot*, it can be harmful.

The *roots* of *Good King Henry* can be fed to sheep to cure them of coughs.

Place a *lump of sugar* in 1 teaspoonful of *vinegar*, and when the sugar has absorbed all the vinegar suck out the vinegar slowly.

Tisane, an infusion of herbs taken as tea, sweetened with *honey* will relieve catarrh and coughs.

Eat plenty of *cherries*.

Drink *elderberry wine*.

Raspberry vinegar: Bruise 2 lb. *raspberries*, place in a bowl, pour 1½ pints *vinegar* over them and allow to stand for 48 hours. Keep in a warm place and cover with a cloth. When the time is up, strain through a muslin bag and collect the juice in an enamelled saucepan. Add 1 lb. *sugar* to each pint liquid and stir until the sugar dissolves, then bring to the boil and simmer gently. As scum appears, skim until the liquid is clear. Allow to cool and bottle. Seal the corks with wax to ensure that the bottles are perfectly airtight until needed. Take a wineglassful of this three times a day.

Put together in a bottle 6 oz. *cod liver oil*, 2 oz. *glycerine*, 6 oz. *honey*, and the *juice* of 4 *lemons*. Shake the mixture well before taking 1 tablespoonful three times a day.

CRAMP

To relieve cramp, the affected part should be rubbed with *yarrow*.

Tie bands of *periwinkle* round the affected part. *Note*: *Periwinkle* is poisonous if eaten.

CROUP

Rue tea will provide relief, but do not take too much as it can make you ill.

CUTS

Bind on *leaves of comfrey* to heal a cut. *Marigold leaves* may also be used in this manner.

Rub the affected part directly with *yarrow*.

Lily of the valley leaves can be used to draw any septic cuts, and when the cut is clean they will help the flesh to heal quickly. *Note*: *Lily of the valley* is poisonous if eaten.

Use a freshly cut piece of *horseradish root* on cuts to prevent them becoming septic.

DANDRUFF

Wash the hair regularly with the liquid from an infusion of *rosemary*.

DEAFNESS

Insert the core of a *roast onion* into the ear.

Cook a *hedgehog* and apply its *fat* to the inside of the ear.

DIARRHOEA

In April take up the *root of cinquefoil*, remove the outer bark and dry it. Then make a decoction by boiling 2 oz. of the root in 1 quart water until the liquid is reduced to 1 pint. A wineglassful taken every 2 hours is a certain cure.

The *dried leafy tops of cinquefoil* can be steeped in water for 15 minutes and the liquid taken three times a day as a remedy for diarrhoea.

Make a decoction from the *crushed root of comfrey* and take in a wineglass three times a day to cure diarrhoea and dysentery.

DIGESTION

In order to assist with the digestion of any rich food take a small quantity of *horseradish root* after the meal.

DYSENTERY

Take a decoction of *crushed comfrey root* in a wineglass three times a day.

ECZEMA

Drink *dandelion tea*, and bathe the affected part with the cold tea.

EPILEPSY

Chop the *stems and leaves of mistletoe* into small pieces and boil, then drink the water in which the mistletoe was boiled. Take care not to include mistletoe berries in the brew, they are poisonous.

EYES

A decoction of *camomile* used as a compress will bring relief to tired eyes. *Note*: Camomile can be harmful if too much is taken internally.

Use cold *dandelion tea* to bathe sore eyes. A decoction of *fennel* is also very effective, as is cold *chickweed tea*.

For those with weak eyes, make a lotion by infusing a handful of *speedwell* in ½ pint boiling water. Strain, and use the water to bathe the eyes night and morning.

In early summer take some *common garden snails*, wipe them clean and prick with a needle through their shells. Hang them up in a fine unstarched cloth. Add the liquid that drops from them to an equal quantity of *olive oil*, and use as eye-drops, applying one drop twice each day. Shake the bottle well before use.

Keep *rain water* that falls on Ascension day to cure sore eyes.

Take a handful of *eye-bright flowers* and steep in boiling water. Leave to cool, strain, and bathe the affected eyes.

FEET

Bathe tired feet in an infusion of *lavender*.

FEVER

A decoction made from *borage* will help to reduce a fever.

Steep the fresh *flowers of meadowsweet* in *rain water* for 24 hours, then boil the liquid for 5 minutes and take a small quantity every 2 hours.

An infusion of *sorrel* will help to reduce a fever.

Make a decoction from the *dried leaves of wormwood* gathered in the late summer and take a wineglassful every 4 hours.

Yarrow tea will promote perspiration, which can help to reduce a fever. Eating *garlic* has the same effect.

FINGERS

To cure a gathered or festering finger make a paste of *soap* and *sugar* and bind this on to the affected part.

FLATULENCE

Take 2 oz. *scraped horseradish*, ½ oz. *mustard seed* and a pinch of *salt*, and cover with *boiling vinegar*. Leave to steep for 24 hours, strain and bottle. When needed, mix 1 teaspoonful in a glass of hot water and sip slowly.

A decoction made from the *seeds of dill* makes a soothing mixture for the relief of flatulence.

An infusion of *calamint* or *sweet cicely* (*myrrh*) will bring relief.

Rue tea or *clover tea* taken after a heavy meal will help to prevent flatulence. Too much *rue tea*, however, can make you ill.

FRECKLES

To get rid of freckles apply *ointment* made of *cowslip flowers*. Crush and boil the flowers in *unsalted lard* for ½ hour. The liquid should then be strained through a fine cloth into clean jars and allowed to set before tying down.

Wash well with *elderflower water* when the *moon* is *waning*. To make elderflower water pack the flowers in a large jug or other container and pour over them ½ gallon boiling water. Cover with a cloth so that none of the steam can escape. Leave to stand for 24 hours, strain and bottle. *Note*: Raw *elder seeds* are emetically poisonous.

GALLSTONES

Silverweed tea will help to dispel gallstones.

GOUT

Apply the *bruised leaves* and *stems of tansy* in the form of a poultice to the affected part. Bandage lightly and change the dressing frequently.

Take a decoction of the *dried roots* of either *chicory* or *couchgrass* to relieve gout.

HAIR

An infusion of the *dried leaves* and *flowers of rosemary* mixed with a little *borax* used when washing and rubbed into the scalp each day will promote healthy and strong growth and will add lustre to your hair.

To make a hair rinse: Take a double handful of *fresh herbs* and place in a jug or other container. Then pour 1 quart boiling water over them. The container should be covered with a cloth to prevent the steam escaping. When cool strain through a double layer of muslin. Use *camomile* for fair hair, *sage and rosemary* for dark hair.

Hair tonic: Infuse equal portions of *camomile flowers, rosemary, bay, sage* and *southernwood* in 1 quart boiling water. Keep covered during the infusion, and when cool, bottle. This lotion should be regularly massaged into the scalp. It is an excellent tonic and will help to strengthen and feed the roots.

A wash to stop hair falling out: Boil ¼ oz. *unprepared tobacco leaves*, 2 oz. *rosemary leaves* and 2 oz. *box leaves* in 1 quart water, well covered, for 20 minutes. Strain and apply cold to the roots of the hair from time to time during the summer months.

For baldness: Sleep in a cap made of ivy leaves. *Note*: *Ground ivy berries* are poisonous to children if eaten.

HANDS

To make rough or sore hands smooth, rub them well with *elder-flower cream* (see p. 168).

HEADACHES

Tea made from verbena will help to get rid of persistent, nagging headaches.

Dry leaves of *betony*, grind them to a powder and take as a safeguard against headaches.

Elderflower water (see p. 173) will provide relief, as will *marjoram* or *rosemary tea*. *Note*: Raw *elder seeds* are emetically poisonous.

Wear an *adder skin* in your hat as a safeguard against headaches.

HEART

A tea made from the *leaves* and *flowers* of *motherwort* can be used as a stimulant for the heart.

A decoction made from *marigold flowers* will provide a gentle stimulant.

HEAT LUMPS

Elderflower cream (see p. 168) is good for heat lumps.

HICCOUGHS

A decoction made from *dill seeds* and then taken 1 teaspoonful at a time will dispel hiccoughs in a baby.

Tea made from the *roots* and *leaves of willow herb* will help to dispel a severe attack of hiccoughs.

INDIGESTION

Steep a handful of *mint leaves* in a small quantity of *alcohol – gin* can be used – and leave until the leaves have yielded all their oil and juice. Take a few drops of the liquid in a wineglassful of hot water.

Sage tea is a gentle cure for indigestion.

INFECTIOUS DISEASES

Burn the *dried tops* of *sage leaves* to *disinfect* a sickroom and dispel the germs from any infectious diseases.

When in contact with a person suffering from an infectious disease, hold a *sprig of angelica* in your mouth, or chew a *clove of garlic* or *thyme leaves* to ward off germs.

A block of *camphor* tied round the neck will keep off infectious diseases.

INFLAMMATION

Poultices to be applied directly to the affected parts can be made from *angelica stems and leaves, linseed*, the leaves of *Good King Henry*, or the *dried leaves of marjoram*.

Marigold leaves can be applied fresh to the affected part for relief.

Cover the inflamed area with an ointment made from *bruised* and *chopped periwinkle leaves* and *unsalted lard*. The two ingredients should be heated together over a slow heat for at least 1 hour. *Note*: Periwinkle is poisonous when eaten.

INFLUENZA

A strong infusion made from *dried elderflowers* flavoured with *mint* and sweetened with *honey*, taken every 4 hours, will bring relief to influenza sufferers.

JAUNDICE

A decoction made from 1 oz. *chicory root* to 1 pint boiling water, taken in a small wineglass every 2 hours, will be effective in the cure of jaundice.

KIDNEYS

To purify the kidneys take a handful of *wild carrot seeds* and a few *roots*, bring slowly to the boil in 1 pint water, and leave to cool. Strain through muslin and drink the infusion in small doses, too much may make you ill.

There are a number of *teas* made from the following herbs that have the beneficial effect of 'flushing' the kidneys: *parsley, clover, couchgrass* and *yarrow*. An infusion made from *bilberries* is also effective.

LIVER

An infusion of either the *dried or fresh leaves* of *lady's mantle* taken four times a day in a wineglass is valuable for all liver troubles.

Sage tea will tone up the liver.

An infusion made from *wild carrot seeds* and *roots* (see above, under KIDNEYS) will purify the liver, but take care not to take too much as it may make you ill.

MOUTH

Use an infusion of *thyme* as a gargle and to sweeten the breath.

NERVES

Dry and powder the *leaves of basil* and take as snuff.

A decoction made from *basil* is an excellent tonic for the nerves. Take a wineglassful twice a day.

Clover tea taken once a day from time to time will guard against all manner of nervous disorders.

A decoction made from the *leaves of mistletoe* grown on an *oak tree* will tone up the nerves and assist circulation of the blood if taken night and morning. Take care not to include any mistletoe berries; they are poisonous.

Boil 1 oz. *tansy leaves* in 1 pint water for 10 minutes. Take ½ teacupful to steady nerves. *Note*: An overdose of an infusion of tansy can be poisonous.

An infusion of 1 oz. *dried camomile flowers* to 1 pint boiling water will help to calm those of a nervous disposition, but do not take too much as it can be harmful.

NOSEBLEED

Take a handful of *fresh-gathered stinging nettles* and bruise in a mortar with as much water as will hang on the nettles when they are dipped in water; when thoroughly reduced to a pulp, extract the juice by wringing out in a cloth and inject into the nose.

OBESITY

Regularly eat any part of *fennel* to reduce weight.

Chickweed tea will help to prevent obesity.

PNEUMONIA

Cover the chest with a *poultice* made from *cow dung*.

RHEUMATISM

Treat with a *hot poultice* made from *rotten apples*.

Wrap an *adder skin* round the affected parts.

Carry a *hare's foot* in your pocket.

Carry a *mole's foot* tied round the neck.

There are three *teas* which are beneficial to all sufferers from rheumatism: tea made from *hyssop and white horehound* in equal parts, *couchgrass tea* and *nettle tea*.

A drastic but effective method of obtaining relief is by *whipping* the affected part with a bunch of old *nettles*.

A decoction made from the *root of chicory* will relieve rheumatic pains, as will *plasters* and *poultices* made from the *leaves of belladonna or tansy*. *Note*: Belladona can be fatally poisonous if eaten.

The *leaves of ground elder* should be rubbed on to the affected part several times a day. *Note*: Raw *elder seeds* are emetically poisonous.

Infuse *rosemary flowers* in hot water and drink twice a day.

Wear an *eelskin garter* as a protection against rheumatism and cramp.

RINGWORM

Rub the affected part with the juice from *crushed celandines*. This is also good for stopping an itch. *Note*: *Celandines* are poisonous when eaten.

SICKNESS

Wormwood tea will quickly clear up a bilious attack.

Drink several glasses of *dandelion tea* during the day. To make the tea infuse 1 oz. *dandelion petals* in 1 pint boiling water for 10 minutes; then strain and sweeten with *honey*.

SINUSITIS

Steep a jugful of *lavender* in boiling water and inhale the steaming vapour.

SKIN

Mix equal parts of *flowers of sulphur* and *homemade unsalted lard* to a smooth paste. This is a quick cure for most skin disorders and can be used at once.

Steep the *peel* from 2 *lemons* in a small quantity of boiling water. When cold, add 2 oz. *glycerine* and 1 oz. *powdered borax* to the liquid and bottle. This lotion is ready for use immediately.

Buttercup ointment (see p. 167) is good for all kinds of skin disorders. *Note*: *Buttercups* are poisonous if taken internally.

SLEEP

The dried leaves of *lady's mantle* made into a pillow will induce sleep.

SORES

Apply the *leaves of lady's mantle* directly on to the sore and bandage lightly.

Take 1 lb. *unsalted leaf-lard* and 2 handfuls each of *elder flowers, groundsel* and *dried rosemary flowers*. Place all in an earthenware pot, bring to the boil in the oven, and simmer for ½ hour. Strain and place in pots. This can be stored, but it is better to use it fresh. *Note*: *Groundsel* is poisonous if eaten.

Make an ointment from 1 lb. *unsalted leaf-lard* and 1 lb. *fully opened elder flowers*. Put a layer of lard and a layer of flowers alternately in a stone or earthenware jar. Place the vessel in a warm oven. When the lard has melted stir with a wooden spoon and press the flowers against the sides of the jar. Simmer on top of the oven for ½ hour, stirring all the time. Strain through muslin and store in glass or stone pots. *Note*: Raw *elder seeds* are emetically poisonous.

SORE THROATS

Simmer 1 small glassful *port wine*, 1 tablespoonful *chilli vinegar*, 6 *sage leaves* and 1 dessertspoonful *honey* all together for 5 minutes and then use the liquid as a gargle.

Mulberry water: Bruise 1 lb. *mulberries* with 6 oz. *brown sugar*; add 1 pint water, mix, and filter through a fine sieve. Sip slowly.

Take 2 oz. *barberries* and 1 oz. *violets* (these can be dried) and infuse in 1 quart boiling water for 20 minutes. Sweeten with *honey*. Strain off the liquid and drink several glasses a day. *Strawberries*, *blackcurrants* or *raspberries* may be added in season.

Take a *sock* straight from the foot and wrap it lightly round the neck.

Take a decoction of *white horehound* as required to ease a sore throat.

Relief will come to a sore throat from taking a small wineglassful every 2 hours of an infusion made from 1 oz. *self heal* to 1 pint boiling water sweetened with *honey*.

Stinging nettle tea brings comfort to a sore throat.

Take a tablespoonful of warmed *goose-grease* three times a day.

Take as often as required a cup of *blackcurrant tea*, made by pouring boiling water over blackcurrant jam.

SPRAINS

Rub the affected part well with *bruised aconite leaves*, then apply as a plaster. *Note*: *Aconite* is fatally poisonous if eaten.

Rub the area affected by the sprain with the *flowers of arnica*.

Bruise a handful of *sage leaves* and boil them in 1 gill *vinegar* for 5 minutes. Apply this to the affected part in a folded napkin as hot as can be borne.

Mix together 4 oz. *ammonia*, 4 oz. *spirit of wine* and 4 oz. *rose-water*. Apply regularly to the affected part.

Green oils: Mix well together 2½ oz. *turpentine*, 1¼ oz. *oil of origanum* and 7½ oz. *oil of green oil*. Smooth gently on the affected part and allow the mixture to be absorbed. Store in a bottle.

Take equal parts of *glycerine* and *castor oil* and a little *melted beeswax*. Mix well together and rub on to the affected part.

Embrocation (poultice): Take 1 egg and ½ pint *turpentine*. Place in a bottle and shake until the mixture becomes creamy. Then add 1 pint *vinegar*, a little at a time, and shake. After shaking well, add 1 tablespoonful *liquid ammonia*. This embrocation will keep for a long time in a well corked bottle.

Liniment: Take 1 part *vinegar*, 1 part *turpentine*, 1 *egg* and a piece of *camphor*. Mix all the ingredients together in a bottle, shaking well, until the resulting liquid is creamy. It is then ready for use.

Splint for sprains: Gather the large *leaves of comfrey* and bind around the arm or leg. As the leaves dry they become a very firm splint.

STINGS

Rub *bee stings* with the *bruised leaves of alecost*.

Rub *bee* or *wasp stings* with the *bruised leaves of summer savory.*

For *nettle stings,* spit on the affected part and bind a *dock leaf* round it.

STOMACH UPSETS

To quell an upset stomach take 1 tablespoonful of a decoction made from *verbena* every 2 hours until relief is obtained.

Elderflower water (see p. 173) and *fennel tea* are also recommended for this complaint. *Note*: Raw *elder seeds* are emetically poisonous.

SWELLINGS

Make a poultice from the *flowers of camomile* and apply frequently to the affected part.

TEETH

To keep teeth healthy, rub them well with a *leaf of sage* after meals.

To relieve toothache carry a *potato* or a *double hazelnut* in your pocket.

Let the sufferer from toothache fill his mouth with *cold spring water* and sit himself beside the fireplace till the water boils!

For toothache bake several large *lily leaves* in the oven and apply to the face, or *chew cloves.*

THRUSH

To cure thrush in a child, find an *ash tree* growing beside a *running stream* and tie a *thread* round one of the twigs, tying *three knots.* Repeat the operation for the next two days, then remove the string and pass it through the child's mouth. This is most effective if the operation is carried out by a seventh son or a seventh daughter.

TIREDNESS

Three handfuls of *primroses* or *cowslips* in a *hot bath* provides relief.

Borage added to any drink will act as a stimulant.

ULCERS

Silverweed tea will calm an ulcer.

VARICOSE VEINS

Tea made from the *flowers and leaves* of the *daisy* will help to dispel varicose veins.

WARTS

Rub the warts with the *downy inside* of a *broad bean pod* and chant this rhyme, 'As this bean shell rots away, so my warts shall soon decay.'

Place three drops of *blood* from a wart on an *elder leaf* and bury it in the earth; as the leaf rots so the warts will disappear.

Touch each wart with a separate *pea pod*. Then wrap the pods up in paper and bury them in the ground. As the pods rot, so the warts will disappear. The same applies to a *freshly cut elder stick* which has been rubbed on the warts.

Rain water collected on a *teasel* will cure warts.

The milk from *thistles*, *marigold* or *crowsfoot* should be rubbed on the warts night and morning.

The *juice of dandelion stalks* is a certain cure for warts.

WHOOPING COUGH

To ease the cough take an infusion of *dried leaves* from the *lungwort* (*Jerusalem cowslip*) three times a day.

Willowherb tea made from the *leaves* and the *root* is known to speed the cure.

Hang the *foot of a mole* round the patient's neck.

Place three *new-laid eggs* in their shells in a pie dish and cover with *vinegar*. When dissolved – and this may take up to 48 hours – mix in ½ lb. *honey*. Take 1 teaspoonful every 4 hours or whenever the cough is troublesome.

Pour 1½ pints cold water on to 2 oz. *wild thyme*. Let it stand for 2 hours, then bring to the boil and simmer for 30 minutes. Strain, add 8 oz. *honey* and serve in a wineglass every 2 hours.

Drown a *trout* in a dish full of cider, then fry the trout. The patient should eat the trout and drink the cider.

WORMS

Take a teaspoonful of *dried and powdered southernwood* mixed with *black treacle* every 4 hours.

Make an infusion of 1 handful of *tansy* to 1 pint boiling water and take night and morning in a teacup on an empty stomach. *Note*: An overdose of an infusion of tansy can be poisonous.

WOUNDS

Comfrey, lady's mantle and *woodruff leaves* can all be used to help heal a wound. Apply the leaves directly to the wound and bind lightly.

WRINKLES

To remove wrinkles apply an ointment made from *crushed cowslip flowers* mixed with *unsalted lard* or *goose-grease*.

PART SIX

Flowers and Trees

Flowers

The Snowdrop, in purest white arraie,
First rears her hedde on Candlemas day;
While the Crocus hastens to the shrine
Of Primrose love on St. Valentine.
Then comes the Daffodil, beside
Our Ladye's Smock at our Ladye-tide.
Aboute St. George, when blue is worn,
The blue Harebells the fields adorne;
Against the day of Holie Cross,
The Crowfoot gilds the flowerie grasse.
When St. Barnabas bright smiles night and daie,
Poor Ragged Robin blossoms in the haie.
The Scarlet Lychnis, the gardens pride,
Flames at St. John the Babtist's tide.
From Visitation to St. Swithen's showers,
The Lilie white reigns Queen of the flowers;
And Poppies, a sanguine mantle spread
For the blood of the Dragon St. Margaret shed.
Then under the wanton Rose, again,
The blushes for Penitent Magdalen,
Till Lammas daie, called August's Wheel,
When the Long Corn stinks of Camamile.
When Mary left us here belowe,
The Virgin's Bower is full of blow;
And became a starre for Batholomew.
The Passion-floure long has blowed,
To betoken us signs of the Holy Roode.
The Michaelmas Daisies, among dede weeds,
Blooms for St. Michael's valourous deeds;
And seems the last of floures that stode,
Till the feast of St. Simon and St. Jude —
Save Mushrooms, and the Fungus race,
That grow till All-Hallow-tide takes place.
Soon the evergreen Laurel alone is greene,
When Charine crownes all learned menne,
The Ive and the Holly Berries are seen,
And Yule Log and Wassaile come round agen.

From an early Calendar of English Flowers

Beautiful flowers are soon picked.

The handsomest flower is not the sweetest.

It is bad soil where no flowers grow.

Nobody is fond of fading flowers.

One flower does not make a garland.

While morning shines gather the flowers.

More grows in the garden than the gardener has sown.

> *The rule of gardening, never forget:*
> *Sow dry, plant wet.*

As is the garden, such is the gardener.

BROOM

An abundance of blossom of broom or furze is an indication of good crops during the ensuing season.

DAISIES

Daisies for simplicity.

Spring has come when you can put your foot on three daisies.

The rose has a summer reign, the daisy never dies.

He's as like as a dock to a daisy.

GORSE

When the gorse is out of bloom, then kissing's out of favour.

ROSES

Roses grow among thorns.

An autumn rose is more delightful than any.

One day causes a rose to open, one day ends its life.

Roses in winter command a high price.

Better to be stung by a nettle than to be pricked by a rose thorn.

Never a rose without a thorn.

> *The rose is red, the violet blue,*
> *Pinks are sweet and so are you.*

Trees

A tree falls not at the first stroke.

A forest is long in growing, but its ashes are made in minutes.

A woman, a dog and a walnut tree, the more you beat them the better they be.

As a tree falls, so shall it lie.

The boughs that bear well hang lowest.

He that loves the tree, loves the branch.

People throw stones only at trees with fruit.

Straight trees can have crooked roots.

Tall trees catch most wind.

Train a tree while it is young.

A tree is no sooner down than everyone runs for a hatchet.

Trees eat but once.

He who plants trees, loves others.

He who plants a walnut tree should not expect to gather the fruit.

You cannot judge a tree by its bark.

If the roots are deep, the tree will not fear the wind.

You may bend a tree while it is a wand.

Shake a tree when the fruit is ripe.

A tree will wither before it falls.

Remove an old tree and it will wither to death.

A tree oft removed will hardly bear good fruit.

As the tree, so the fruit.

St Mathee [24 February] sends the sap up the tree.

Set trees at Hallowtide if you would have them prosper.

Set a tree at Hallowtide and command it to grow;
Set it at Candlemas and entreat it to grow.

APPLE

A bloom on the tree when the apple is ripe,
Is a sure sign to the end of somebody's life.

She went round and round the apple tree till she found a crab
[i.e. she took so long to choose a husband that she found herself
left with an unfortunate partner].

ASH

Ash before oak denotes a wet season.

> *When the ash is before the oak,*
> *Then we shall expect a soak;*
> *But when the oak is before the ash,*
> *Then we'll only get a splash.*
>
> *Buy ash logs, all smooth and grey,*
> *Burn them green or old;*
> *Buy up all that come your way,*
> *They are worth their weight in gold.*

BEECH

Fell beech in summer, oak in winter.

If a beech tree is felled on Midsummer day it will last three times
longer than if it is felled in the winter.

If the beech tree shows a large bud at Christmas there will probably be a moist summer to follow.

BIRCH

Garlands of birch hung on the wall of a house will keep away
demons.

BLACKTHORN

To take blackthorn in blossom into a house presages death to the
occupant.

If you make a crown of blackthorn and bake it in the oven until it has turned to ash, and then scatter it on the fields before dawn on New Year's morning, you can be sure of a good crop.

It is always cold while the blackthorn is in flower.

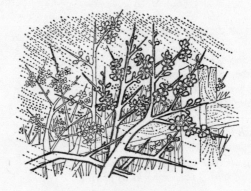

ELM

Elm wood burns like churchyard mould.

When the elm leaf is like a mouse's ear,
Then sow your barley without fear.
When the elm leaves are as big as a farden [farthing],
It is time to plant kidney beans in your garden.
When the elm leaves are as big as a penny,
Plant kidney beans if you mean to have any.
When elm leaves are as big as a shilling,
Plant kidney beans if to plant 'em you're willing.
When the elm leaf is as big as an ox's eye,
Then say 'Hie! Boys! Hie!'

HAWTHORN

If a piece of hawthorn is gathered on Holy Thursday (Maundy Thursday) and kept in the house it will never be struck by lightning because:

Under a thorn
Our Saviour was born.

HAZEL

Hazel has always been regarded as a holy tree, closely associated with fertility; because of this it is frequently used as a divining stick for finding water and precious metals.

HOLLY

Grow holly alongside your house as it is considered to be a protection against thunder and lightning.

IVY

Ivy grown on a house will protect the inmates from witchcraft.

LILAC

It is considered unlucky to bring lilac into the house, particularly white lilac, as death to one of the occupants could follow. However, a single lilac flower with five petals, of any colour, is considered to be very lucky.

OAK

When the oak wears his leaves in October you can expect a hard winter.

Little strokes will fell great oaks.

Oaks can fall when reeds will stand in the storm.

Storms make oaks take deeper roots.

You must look for grass on the top of the oak tree.

Great oaks from little acorns grow.

POPLAR

If anyone was suffering from ague or a fever, they would fasten some of their hair to a poplar and chant, 'Aspen-tree, aspen-tree, I prithee shake and shiver for me'. This was thought to cure them.

ROWAN

Wood from the rowan tree was considered to have the power to ward off evil spirits. It was often built into houses, usually as a supporting beam over a fireplace. It was also used for making plough handles to bring luck to the user and cast off evil spirits from the fields where the plough had been used.

SLOE

When the sloe tree is as white as a sheet,
Sow your barley, fine or wet.

WILLOW

Willows are weak, yet they serve to bind stronger wood.

WOOD FOR BURNING

Beechwood fires burn bright and clear
If the logs are kept a year;
Chestnut's only good they say
If for years 'tis stored away;
Birch and firwood burn too fast,
Blaze too bright and do not last;
But ashwood green and ashwood brown
Are fit for a Queen with a golden crown.

Oaken logs if dry and old
Keep away the winter's cold;
Poplar gives a bitter smoke,
Fills your eyes and makes you choke;
Elmwood burns like churchyard mould,
Even the very flames are cold;
Applewood will scent the room,
Pearwood smells like flowers in bloom;
But ashwood wet and ashwood dry,
A King may warm his slippers by.

Beechwood fires burn bright and clear,
Hornbeam blazes too,
If the logs are kept a year,
To season through and through.

Oak logs will warm you well,
If they are old and dry;
Larchwood and pinewood smell,
But the sparks will fly.

Pine is good, so is yew,
For warmth through wintry days;
But poplar, and willow too,
Take long to dry or blaze.

Birch logs will burn too fast,
Alder scarce at all;
Chestnut logs are good to last,
If cut in the fall.

Holly logs will burn like wax –
You should burn them green;
Elm logs, like smouldering flax,
No flame is seen.

Pear logs and apple logs,
They will scent the room;
Cherry logs across the dogs,
Smell like flowers in bloom.

Dyes from Trees and Bushes

ALDER

From the bark, *tawny red.*

From the catkins, *green.*

From the young shoots, *yellow.*

APPLE and ASH

From the bark, *yellow*.

BILBERRY

From the berries, *purple-black*.

BROOM and GORSE

From the flowers, *yellow*.

ELDER

From the bark, *black*.

From the leaves, *green*.

From the berries, a range of *blues*.

OAK

From the bark, strong *blacks* and *blues*. When mixed with salt this provides the dye for ink.

SLOE

From the berries, *purple*.

WALNUT

From the leaves, the roots and the husk that carries the fruit, *browns*. This dye has been used for the hair for generations.

PART SEVEN

Food and Drink

Food

APPLES

Eat a large apple at midnight on Hallow E'en and you won't catch a cold for twelve months.

Eat an apple going to bed and make the doctor beg his bread.

An apple a day keeps the doctor away.

He pares his apple that will cleanly feed.

An apple, an egg and a nut you may eat after a slut.

A windy year is an apple year.

The fairest apple hangs on the highest branch.

A goodly-looking apple can be rotten at the heart.

Think not every beautiful apple to be good.

An apple pie without cheese is like a kiss without a squeeze.

Lost with an apple, won with a nut.

There is little choice among rotten apples.

A rotten apple spoils its neighbour.

Gather apples for storing during the sinking of the moon.

BUTTER

Boil stones in butter and you may sip the broth.

Butter goes mad twice a year.

Who carries butter on his head should not walk in the sun.

Butter is gold in the morning, silver at noon, lead at night.

That which will not be made butter must be made cheese.

Fair words will butter no parsnips.

CHEESE

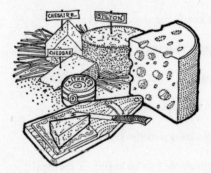

Cheese digests everything but itself.

After cheese comes nothing.

Make good cheese if you make any.

Toasted cheese hath no master.

A rainy Easter brings a cheese year.

CRESS

Eat cress and learn more wit.

FIGS

Peel a fig for your friend and a peach for your enemy.

HAWS

Many haws, many snows.

HONEY

A little gall spoils a great deal of honey.

Mouth of honey, heart of gall.

Honey and wax, sweetness and light.

Honey can come from weeds.

He who would gather honey must bear the sting of bees.

If you daub yourself with honey you will soon be covered with flies.

A drop of honey catches more flies than a barrel of vinegar.

He who deals with honey licks his fingers.

MEAT

God sendeth and giveth both mouth and meat.

To make tough meat tender, wrap it in sorrel leaves when cooking.

NUTS

Nuts are given to us, but we must crack them ourselves.

PEARS

A pear year is a dear year.

After a pear, wine or a priest.

The best pears fall for the pigs.

Country 'Receipts'

God sends meat, but the Devil sends cooks.

A cook is known by his knife.

Cooks are not to be taught in their own kitchens.

Too many cooks spoil the broth.

A bad cook licks his own fingers.

Hunger is the best cook.

The following recipes are included to recall the sort of food eaten by all classes of countryfolk, from the occupants of the 'grand' houses to the most humble cottagers.

Few of these recipes are of practical use today as they were intended for open-hearth cooking. When an oven is mentioned, it could mean either a 'Dutch' oven, which was stood in front of the fire and reflected the heat from its curved back plate on to the meats or other items to be cooked, or a bread oven, which was usually built into the thick wall that enclosed the open hearth. The bread oven was heated by burning faggots of wood inside the oven itself and when all was well burnt the ashes were drawn out with a long-handled rake. The slab floor of the oven was then swabbed with a mop made of old rags fixed to the end of a peel. The peel would be used to insert and remove the bread, cakes, pies, puddings and meats to be baked in the oven. In country districts the main source of heat for the open hearths was wood, and/or peat when this was readily available.

In most country homes a day was set apart each week for all the baking and the cooking to be done for the family for the week. This was the case, up to fifty years ago, in my wife's home – an isolated Herefordshire farmhouse, where much of the cooking was done on an open hearth.

Labour was cheap, and in the kitchens of the big houses, plentiful, so it was in no way a problem to go through the lengthy preparations necessary for such dishes as pies made from larks or other small birds.

I am grateful to have had the loan from time to time of old 'receipt' books that have been laboriously and immaculately written down and handed on from mothers to daughters over many generations.

Oven settings and temperatures were unheard of, and testing was done with a fork or by tasting, coupled with a good deal of native wit.

SAVOURY

BACON PUDDING

Make a stiff dough with 1 lb. *flour*, 7 oz. *suet* and a little water. Roll this dough out on a floured board to ½ in. thickness, then cover with chopped *bacon* and *onions*, and season with *salt, pepper* and chopped *sage*. Roll up the pastry, tie in a pudding cloth, and boil for 2 – 2½ hours.

BACON ROLL (FILL-BELLY)

Spread *suet pastry* with chopped *bacon*. Roll and seal the edges. Boil in a scalded cloth and eat with *mashed potatoes*.

EEL PIE

Cut a good-sized *eel* into pieces and place in a pan with *mixed herbs*, chopped *onion*, and *pepper* and *salt* to taste. Cover with *stock*. Cook gently until the flesh can be removed from the bones. Place the flesh in a pie dish and add a squeeze of *lemon* and *stock* to just cover. Cover with *short pastry* and bake in a hot oven for ¾ hour.

FAGGOTS

Mince 1 lb. *pig's liver*, 1 *pig's heart*, the *lungs*, the *skirt* (after the chitterlings have been removed), 1½ lb. *onions* and 2 oz. *sage leaves*. To this mixture add a 2 lb. *loaf* that has been *soaked in water or stock* and squeezed almost dry, and *salt* and *pepper* to taste. Roll the mixture into balls with hands that have been dipped in water, place in rows in a pan, and cover each faggot with a square of *caul*, or wrap each one completely. Bake in a hot oven for 1–1½ hours.

FILL-BELLY PASTRY

Boil 1 pint *wheat* in water. When cooked, add 1 lb. *dried fruit*, ½ lb. chopped *suet*, 1 lb. *brown sugar*, an *apple* chopped into small pieces, with the juice and grated rind of 1 *lemon*. Mix all well together and use as a filling for pasties.

GIBLET PIE

Procure two sets of *goose giblets* (ready-cleaned if possible). Parboil them in water with a little *salt* for about 6 minutes, then wash and drain them and leave them to cool in a sieve.

Next, place the giblets in a stew pan with *carrots*, *celery* and an *onion* stuck with 6 *cloves*, seasoned with a bouquet of *parsley*, *thyme*, *marjoram*, *basil*, *spring onions* and a few *peppercorns*. Moisten with *stock* with a little *catsup* added and stew the giblets very slowly over a fire for about 1½ – 2 hours.

When the giblets are done, drain them in a sieve. Wash and cut them into pieces measuring about 2 inches; cut the livers and gizzards smaller. Place everything in a pie dish already lined with seasoned *collops of beef*. With the stock from the giblets make some sauce, well boiled and free from all grease and impurities, and boiled down to a proper consistency. Pour it into the pie, add *hard-boiled eggs* and cover with *pastry*. Bake for 1¼ hours and serve.

GREEN GOOSE

Draw the *goose*, pick off all the stubble feathers, scald the legs, rub off the skin with a cloth, cut off the tips of the feet and twist the legs round, so as to let the webs of the feet rest flat upon the thighs. Then truss the goose in the ordinary way as directed for pheasants (see p. 209). Place the goose on a spit and roast before a brisk fire for about ¾ hour; when done dish it up with some *watercress* around it and *gravy* under.

Ducklings are roasted and served in the same way.

GROUSE PIE

Pick and draw two or three *young grouse*. Cut off the wings and legs and tuck the drumsticks in through a slit made under the thigh. Singe the birds over a charcoal flame, then split them in half. Season and fry them in a little *butter* until half done.

Simultaneously with this part of the operation, prepare some *collops of beef*. Season, fry them and place them in the bottom of a pie dish. Add chopped *mushrooms, parsley, shallots* and 1 table-spoonful *Worcester sauce* (see p. 214). Place the fried halves of grouse in neat order on this, add a little more seasoning and some yolks of *hard-boiled eggs*; then moisten with *gravy* with a little *salt* added, so that it all reaches up the sides of the pie dish. Cover with *puff pastry*, and bake for about 1¼ hours.

GUINEA FOWL

When two of these are served for a dish, one should be *larded* and the other covered with a layer of *bacon*. Roast them before a brisk fire for about 20 minutes. *Glaze* and dish up with *watercress*, and *gravy* poured under; hand round *bread sauce*.

HARE – JUGGED

Parboil 1 lb. *streaky bacon* for 20 minutes to extract the salt. Cut into 1 inch squares, fry these in a stew pan, then add the *hare* cut into joints. Fry these until brown, shake in 6 oz. *flour*, moisten with 1 quart *stock*, 2 glassfuls *port wine* and a small quantity of *catsup*. Add 8 rather small *onions*, 1 lb. of the *red part* of *carrots*, cut into neatly-shaped 1 inch squares, ½ lb. *mushrooms*, a garnished faggot of *parsley, pepper* and *salt*.

Stir all together over the fire until it boils and then set it by the side to simmer until the pieces of hare are tender. Remove the scum, and pour off the sauce into another stew pan, to be further reduced by boiling, if necessary, to give it a good consistency; then strain it back into the jugged hare.

At the last moment add 1 glassful *port wine* and 4 oz. *currant jelly*. Heat up and serve.

HARE – ROAST

Skin and draw the *hare*, leaving on the ears, which must be scalded and the hairs scraped off; pick out the eyes and cut off the feet or pads just above the first joint; wipe the hare with a clean cloth, and cut the sinews at the back of the hindquarters and below the forelegs.

Prepare some *veal or hare stuffing* (see p. 213) and next recipe respectively) and fill the paunch with it; sew this up with string, or fasten it with a wooden skewer. Then draw the legs under as if the hare were in a sitting posture, set the head between the shoulders, and stick a small skewer through them, running it through the neck also to secure its position. Gather the forelegs up under the paunch and run another skewer through them; then take a yard of string, fold it in two, placing the centre of the string on the breast of the hare, and bring both ends over the skewer; cross the string over both ends of the other skewer and fasten it over the back.

Spit the hare and roast it in front of a brisk fire for about ¾ hour, frequently basting with *butter or dripping*. Five minutes before taking the hare up, throw on a little *salt*, shake some *flour* over it with the dredger, and baste it with some *fresh butter*. When this froths up and the hare has acquired a rich brown crust, take it off the spit, dish it up with *watercress* round it and *brown gravy* under, and hand round *redcurrant jelly*.

HARE STUFFING

Cut up the *liver*, *heart* and *lights* of a *hare*, and fry them with an equal quantity of *ham or bacon*, seasoned with *mushrooms*, *parsley*, *shallots*, *salt*, *pepper* and *nutmeg*. When slightly browned, pound all together with about 2 oz. *breadcrumbs* and 1 whole *egg* in a mortar. When the ingredients have been well pulverized into a smooth paste the mixture can be used for stuffing hares and rabbits.

HASLET

Mix together 1 lb. *pork pieces* after trimming the bacon flitches, 1 lb. soaked *breadcrumbs*, 1 oz. chopped *sage*, 2 good *onions*, *pepper* and *salt* to taste. Wrap this mixture in *caul* and bake in a hot oven until done, approximately 1 hour.

KETTLE BROTH

Spread a thick slice of *bread* with *dripping* and season with *salt* and *pepper* to taste; cut them up into cubes and place them in a basin. Add boiling water until the cubes just float and eat as quickly as possible.

LAMB TAIL PIE

Scald the *lambs' tails* (3 parts boiling water, 1 part cold) and re- move all wool. Place the tails, some *carrots* and some *onions* in sufficient *stock* to cover and simmer over a low heat until the tails are tender. Then roll each tail in chopped *parsley* and place in a pie dish with *hard-boiled eggs* (one per person). Add a little *stock*, cover with *short pastry*, brush with *egg* and bake in a moderately hot oven until the crust is golden brown.

LARD

Cut all spare *back fat* into ¾ inch cubes and place in a pan over a slow heat. Cut up likewise the thick *caul* from inside the pig and add these cubes to the pan when the back fat is floating in its own liquid.

Continue to cook until the mixture is just simmering. Simmer until the cubes have shrunk to about a quarter of their original size, then increase the heat, stirring all the time, until all the fat is crisp. It should then be removed from the pan and pressed with a wooden mould in a colander and the liquid returned to the pan, where it should be brought to the boil and held for 5 minutes before pouring the fat into basins to set. A little *salt* should be added at the last boiling stage.

If you want to flavour the lard with *rosemary*, add the bruised leaves during the quick-boiling period and leave them in the lard while it sets in the basins.

LEEK PIE

Chop the *leek* into ½-inch thick rings, place in a saucepan, sprinkle with *salt* and pour over boiling water to cover. Leave the leeks to steep for 5 minutes and then drain.

Slice up some rashers of *fat bacon*, add *pepper* and *salt* to taste, add the chopped rashers to the leeks, and cover again with boiling water. Place over a low heat and cook until the leeks are tender.

Turn all into a baking dish, cover with a *shortcrust pastry*, glaze with *milk*, and bake in a moderate oven until the pastry is a golden brown, then remove the crust and drain off the water.

Add 2 *eggs* beaten with a little *milk*, and *pepper* and *salt* to season; bake again in a moderate oven until the beaten eggs have set.

MUTTON PIES

Take 1 lb. *lean mutton* and cut into small squares, season with chopped *mushrooms, parsley, shallots, pepper* and *salt* and a little stock and mix all together in a basin. Next, line some tartlet or patty pans with *shortcrust pastry* made without sugar. Fill these with some of the prepared meat, cover them with pastry, press and pinch them round the edge, and *egg* them over. Make a small hole in the top for ventilation to prevent them bursting whilst baking. Cook them in the oven on a baking sheet for about 20 minutes. When done dish them up on a napkin.

Note: Small patties made as directed above, filled with *chicken, veal and ham*, any kind of *meat or game*, or any of the great variety of preparations for making *croquettes*, make an agreeable change for the dinner table, and are also calculated to become favourite additions to picnics and race-course luncheons, and to the sportsman's basket.

PARTRIDGE PIE

Truss loosely, singe, and divide into halves 3 *young partridges*. *Season* and fry them in a little *butter*. Line a pie dish with thin *collops of veal* and *half-boiled bacon*; season with chopped *mushrooms, parsley, pepper* and *salt*.

Pour 1 gill *onion sauce* over the veal, etc., then place the halves of partridges neatly in the pie dish, repeat the seasoning, pour over more onion sauce and add the *yolks* of some *hard-boiled eggs*. Cover with *pastry* and bake for about 1¼ hours. Pour in a little good *gravy* before serving.

PARTRIDGES – ROAST

These should be trussed, roasted and served in the same manner as *pheasants*. Sometimes, for the sake of variety, both pheasants and partridges can be *larded*, but the practice is not generally liked.

PEAHENS

Truss these in the same way as for pheasants, except that the head must be left on, adhering to the skin of the breast, and fastened at the side of the thigh. Let the *peahen* be closely *larded* all over the breast and roasted before a moderate fire for about 1 hour. When nearly done *glaze* the larding. On removing the fowl from the fire, dish up with *watercress*, pour some *gravy* under and serve with *bread sauce*.

PHEASANT – ROAST

Draw the *pheasant* by making a small opening at the vent. Make an incision along the back part of the neck, loosen the pouch, etc., with the fingers, and then remove it. Singe the body of the pheasant and its legs over the flames of a charcoal fire, or with a piece of lighted paper. Rub the scaly cuticle off the legs with a cloth; trim away the claws and spurs; cut off the neck close to the back, leaving the skin of the breast entire; wipe the pheasant clean, and then truss it in the following manner:

Place the pheasant upon its breast, run a trussing needle and string through the left pinion (the wings having been removed); then turn the bird over on to its back, and place the thumb and forefinger of the left hand across the breast, holding the legs erect; thrust the needle through the middle joint of both thighs, draw it out, and then pass it through the other pinion, and fasten the strings at the back. Next, pass the needle through the hollow of the back, just below the thighs, thrust it through the legs and body again, and tie the strings tightly. This will give it the appearance of plumpness.

Spit and roast the pheasant before a brisk fire for about ½ hour, *basting* it frequently. When done, send to table with *brown gravy* under it and *bread sauce* separately in a boat.

PIE OF SMALL BIRDS

The birds best suited to this purpose are *fieldfares*, *blackbirds* and *larks*. These birds are only fit for table during the months of November, December and January, and they are at their best during frosty weather.

The birds intended for the pie should be stuffed with the following preparations:

Soak the crumbs of a *French roll* in a little *milk* and put it in a stew pan with 2 oz. *butter*, a little grated *lemon peel*, *shallots*, chopped *parsley*, *nutmeg*, *pepper* and *salt*, a pinch of *aromatic herbs* and 3 *egg yolks*. Stir this over the fire until it becomes a compact paste, and use it to fill the insides of the birds.

Line the bottom of a pie dish with fried *collops of beef*, and place thereon the birds in neat order. Pour on some *fine herbs sauce*, add *hard-boiled eggs*, cover with *puff pastry* and bake the pie for 1¼ hours.

PIGEON PIE

Line the bottom of a pie dish with small *collops of lean steak*, previously fried brown. Season with chopped *mushrooms*, *parsley*, *shallots* and *salt*. Pour ½ pint *gravy* and a little *catsup* into the pan the meat has been fried in, and then pour this over the contents of the dish. Add the yolks of 6 *hard-boiled eggs*, *plover's eggs* when in season, and cover all with *puff pastry*. Bake in a moderate oven for about 1¼ hours.

PIGEON – ROAST

Truss the *pigeons* with thin layers of *fat bacon* and place a *vine leaf* over the breast; roast the birds for about 20 minutes, and when done dish them up with a *sauce* made from the *livers* in the manner directed for making liver sauce for rabbits (see p. 211).

QUAILS – ROAST

Draw and truss in the manner directed for pheasants (see p. 209). Slice some thin squares of *fat bacon* just large enough to cover a quail, spread a *vine leaf* over each bird, trim the leaves to the size of the birds and tie them neatly to the breasts. Run an iron skewer through the quails, fasten this on to a spit and roast them before a brisk fire for about ¼ hour. Dish them up with *watercress* round them and *gravy* under them.

RABBIT – ROAST

Truss *rabbits* in the same manner as hares (see p. 206), then spit-roast them before a rather brisk fire, basting frequently. Ten minutes before taking them up, baste the rabbits with the following preparation:

Mix 1 gill *cream* with 1 tablespoonful *flour*, some chopped *parsley*, 2 *egg yolks*, *pepper*, *salt* and *nutmeg*. Mask the rabbits entirely with this, and as soon as it has dried on them baste with *fresh butter*. This not only adds to the attractive appearance of the rabbits, but it concentrates the gravy, and prevents the rabbits becoming dry, which generally occurs when they are roasted according to the common practice.

When done, take the rabbits up with care, to avoid breaking off the light brown crust which will have formed on them. Before serving, pour some *liver sauce* under them.

Liver sauce is made as follows: boil the *livers*, chop them fine, and put them into a small stew pan with chopped *parsley*, a small piece of *glaze*, a pat of *butter*, 1 spoonful of *Worcester sauce* (see p. 214) *pepper* and *salt*, grated *lemon peel*, *nutmeg* and 1 tablespoonful of *gravy*. Stir this over the fire until it boils and use it as directed above.

ROAST SUCKING PIG

Fill the paunch of the *sucking pig* with *stuffing*, prepared as follows:

Chop fine 4 *onions* and 12 *sage leaves*. Fry these in 2 oz. *butter* over a slow fire for a few minutes, then add ½ lb. *breadcrumbs*, 2 *egg yolks*, *pepper* and *salt*.

And thus, the pig being stuffed, and the paunch sewn up securely, roast it before a brisk fire for about 2 hours, basting it frequently by means of a brush dipped in *olive oil.*

When the pig is cooked and before removing it from the spit, cut off the head and divide the pig into two halves by sawing it straight down the spine. Dish up the pig with brown gravy. To some of the stuffing add the *brains* and a few spoonfuls of *melted butter* and serve this sauce separately.

Alternative stuffing for sucking pig: Scald, peel and scrape 50 *chestnuts* and boil them for about 20 minutes in 1 pint *milk*, a little *butter* and a little *salt.* When nearly done drain and dry the chestnuts and mix them with 1 lb. highly seasoned *sausage meat.*

ROOK PIE

Take the breasts and legs of *young rooks*, allowing at least two per person, and simmer in a good *stock.* When the flesh can be removed from the bones it should be floured and browned in *fat.* Then place in a deep pie dish with slices of *bacon, seasoning,* and sufficient *stock* to cover. Cover with *short pastry* and cook for about 2 hours.

This can be eaten hot or cold.

RUFFS and REEVES

These birds must not be drawn, neither do they require much trussing, being very plump. A small wooden skewer should be run through the thighs and pinions, with a string passed round it, and fastened. Cover the birds with a layer of *bacon* and a *vine leaf.* Run them on to a larkspit, and roast them before a brisk fire for about 20 minutes, basting frequently with *butter*, and set some *toast* under them to receive their drippings. When done dish them up on the pieces of toast, garnish with *watercress*, and pour some *gravy* under them. Serve separately in a boat sauce made from *butter sauce* (melted butter), a piece of *glaze, cayenne pepper* and *lemon juice* well mixed together.

Buntings and *wheatears* are served in the same manner.

SAGE AND ONION STUFFING

Chop up 4 large *onions* and a dozen *sage leaves.* Parboil these together for 2 minutes, drain them, and then put them in a stew pan with about 6 oz. *breadcrumbs*, 2 oz. *butter*, *pepper* and *salt*. Set the stuffing to simmer very gently over a slow fire for about 20 minutes, stirring occasionally. When the onions are nearly done, use this seasoning for stuffing *geese*, *ducks*, or *pork*.

VEAL CAKE

Prepare the following ingredients: about 1½ lb. *veal collops*, ¾ lb. thin slices *ham*, or *streaky bacon* which has been parboiled for 10 minutes to remove some of its saltiness, 4 *hard-boiled eggs*, some *aspic jelly* prepared before from 1 lb. *knuckle of veal*, the *trimmings* from the collops, and a *calf's foot or cow heel*.

Next, take an earthenware pan – such as is commonly used for potting meats – spread or pour on a layer of the aspic jelly, about $\frac{1}{16}$-inch deep, and on this place in neat circles a layer of veal collops. Season with *pepper* and *salt*, chopped *parsley* and *shallots*, and then put on a layer of ham, and on this a layer of hard-boiled eggs cut into neat slices.

Repeat the layers until all the ingredients have been used up. Cover the pan or basin with a stiff *flour and water paste* and bake on a baking sheet containing a little water to prevent the aspic jelly in the cake drying up (an accident which might occur if the oven is too hot).

Bake the pie or cake for 1¼ hours at a moderate heat, and when done set it in a cold place until the next day. It may then be turned out whole on a dish, garnished with *fresh parsley*, and served for breakfast or lunch.

Note: This recipe may be given variety by using *pork*, *beef*, *mutton*, *venison*, *hare*, *poultry*, and all manner of *game*. The addition of an aromatic seasoning is recommended if game is used.

VEAL STUFFING

To ½ lb. *breadcrumbs* add 4 oz. chopped *suet* and 2 *whole eggs*. Season with *parsley*, *thyme*, *marjoram*, *shallots* (the last three in very small quantities), *nutmeg*, *pepper*, and *salt*. Mix well together.

WOODCOCK and SNIPE

To prepare these birds, first pick them entirely, neck and head; then twist the legs at the joints, so as to bring the feet down upon the thighs. Run their bills through the joints and body and fasten a noose with string round the bend in the joints, across the lower part of the breast; bring both ends round the head and tip of the bill, and fasten it on the back.

Cover the birds with layers of *bacon*, and secure them with string. Roast them before the fire for about 25 minutes, basting frequently with *butter or dripping*. Place some *toast* under the birds to receive the drippings from the tail, and when they are cooked dish them up with a piece of the toast under each and *watercress* round them. Serve some plain *butter sauce* (melted butter) separately in a boat.

WORCESTER SAUCE

Mix together 1 pint *malt vinegar*, 2 finely chopped *shallots*, 2 tablespoonfuls *anchovy essence*, 3 tablespoonfuls *walnut ketchup*, 2 tablespoonfuls *soy sauce* and a pinch of *salt*. Place all this in a bottle, well corked down, and give it a good shaking several times a day for a week; then strain and bottle. The longer this sauce is kept the better it is, but it can be used straight away.

SWEET

BEESTINGS CURD

Take 1 pint *beestings milk*, put it in a pie dish, and add a pinch of *salt* and 4 tablespoonfuls *sugar*. Stir well and place in a moderate oven till set.

CATTERN CAKES

Take 2 lb. *dough*, as made for bread, and knead it well with 2 oz. *butter or home-made lard*, 1 oz. *caraway seeds*, 2 oz. *sugar*, and 1 *beaten egg*. Leave to rise in a warm place – usually this takes at least 1 hour – then place in a floured baking tin and bake in a moderate oven.

EASTER CAKES

Rub 3 oz. *butter* and 3 oz. *lard* into 3 oz. *flour*. Stir in 1 oz. *currants*, 1 oz. *chopped peel* and 4 oz. *sugar* and mix to a dough with 2 *beaten eggs*. Roll the mixture out on a floured board and cut into rounds. Bake in a moderate oven until a pale golden brown. These cakes will keep well if stored in an airtight tin.

FIG PUDDING

Chop finely 8 oz. *figs* and mix with 6 oz. grated *suet*, 4 oz. *flour* and a pinch of *salt*. Add sufficient *milk* and *beaten eggs* to make a stiff dough, then turn into a greased pudding basin and steam for 3½ hours.

FIG SUE

Stew ½ lb. *figs* in 1 pint water until they are tender, then pass through a sieve. Warm 2 pints *ale* in a saucepan and add the fig purée. Bring to the boil, stirring all the time, then serve in basins.

HOT CROSS BUNS

Cream together 1 oz. *yeast* and a little *sugar*, then add a spoonful or two of milk and 2 *well-beaten eggs*. Cover them and leave to rise. Warm ½ pint *milk*, weigh 2 lb. *flour*, and add 6 oz. of this with 4 oz. *sugar* to the yeast mixture. Rub 6 oz. *butter* into the remaining flour, and when the yeast mixture has risen and fallen add to it the butter and flour mixture. Mix to a dough and make into buns. Cut a cross on the top of each; thin strips of *pastry* can be placed on the buns to make a cross. Glaze with *egg yolk* and sprinkle with *sugar*. Bake in a hot oven.

MEDICINAL JAM (a mild laxative for children)

Stone 1 lb. *prunes*, chop these and 1 lb. *seedless raisins* together finely, and mix with 2 oz. *blanched whole almonds* and the *kernels* from the prune stones. Let this mixture soak in sufficient water to cover it for 8 hours. Then add 1 lb. *demerara sugar* and 1 *cooking* apple, thinly sliced, and bring to the boil. Cook slowly for ½ hour. Pour into hot jars and seal down immediately.

This is excellent spread on wholemeal bread.

MOTHERING SUNDAY WAFERS

Take 2 tablespoonfuls each of *flour*, *sugar* and *cream* and a small squeeze of *orange juice* and beat all well together. Spread the mixture out very thinly on a well-greased baking sheet in circles about 6 inches in diameter. The mixture should be baked in a hot oven. As soon as they are brown roll them up round the handle of a wooden spoon and leave them to crisp. Cover with *jelly* before eating.

PUDDING PIES

Line some patty pans with *shortcrust pastry* and fill with the following mixture: mix ½ lb. *ground rice* with a little *milk* until it is smooth and creamy. Then add this mixture to 2½ pints *milk* which has been boiled with a *laurel leaf.* Stir all together, then remove from the fire and add ½ lb. *butter*, ½ lb. *sugar*, 8 *eggs*, some *candied peel* and a few *currants*. When this has all been well mixed fill each of the patty pans and bake in a moderate oven.

These are eaten during Lent.

SIMNEL CAKES

Cream 4 oz. *butter* and 4 oz. *brown sugar*. Beat in 2 *eggs*, one at a time. Sift 6 oz. *plain flour* with ½ teaspoonful *baking powder* and stir into the mixture. Add 2 oz. *mixed fruit*, 1½ oz. *orange juice* and some *grated orange rind.* Place this mixture in a 5-inch cake tin lined with two or three layers of greased paper. Roll out 4 oz. *almond paste* to the size of the tin. Shape it carefully to fit. Place in the tin on top of the mixture. Top off with the remainder of the cake mixture and bake in a slow oven for 2½ hours.

SLOE JELLY

Place 3 lb. *sloes* and 1 lb. *apples* in a saucepan, just cover with water and bring to the boil. Continue to cook until they are tender, then strain and rub through a sieve. For each pound of pulp add 1½ lb. *sugar*, and bring to the boil. As soon as it will set (test by dropping a little into a cup of cold water; if it jellifies it is ready) remove from the heat and turn into a mould.

Drink

Thirst is the best spice to drink.

Hang hunger, drown thirst.

He that can master thirst is master of his health.

He who goes to bed thirstily rises healthily.

A thirst departs with drinking.

Go not to the pot for every thirst.

ALE

Ale sellers should not be tale tellers.

As he brews so shall he drink.

Everyone has a penny to spend at the new ale-house.

Good ale is meat, drink and cloth.

He that buys good ale buys nothing else.

When the ale is in, the evil is out.

Beg your balm where you buy your ale.

A quart of ale is a dish for a king.

Bring us no beef for there are many bonys,
But bring us good ale for that goeth down at onys.

Bring us no egges for there are many schelles,
But bring us good ale and gyfe us nothyng ellys.

Back and side go bare, go bare,
Both foot and hand go cold;
But, belly, God send the good ale enough,
Whether it be new or old.

CIDER

Cider on beer makes good cheer,
Beer on cider makes a bad rider.

MILK

It is no use crying over spilt milk.

Wine on milk is desirable, milk on wine, poison.

Milk welcomes wine.

Drink Recipes

CIDER CUP

Mix together 1 quart *cider*, 2 wineglasses *brandy*, 3 tablespoons *sugar* and the juice of ½ *lemon*. Grate some *nutmeg* on to 2 slices of lemon and float the slices on top of the cider cup. Serve cool.

CIDER TODDY

Heat 1 pint *dry cider*, ½ oz. *bruised root ginger* and a twist of *lemon peel* in an enamel saucepan to almost boiling point. Never let it boil. Stir in 2 dessertspoonfuls *honey* and strain into warmed glasses.

COTTAGE CIDER

Gather *windfall apples*, the smaller the better, both of the *dessert* and the *culinary* type, as well as any true cider fruit that may be obtainable. If you like to make a dry cider, then a few *crab apples* will help to provide the necessary astringency.

Place all the fruit in a wooden tub or earthenware vessel and thoroughly bruise it. Cover the bruised and broken fruit with *water* and protect the fruit from dirt and insect pests by covering the vessel with fine muslin, then let it stand for 10 days, giving it a good stir each day.

During this period fermentation will take place, and by the end of the 10 days it should have ceased, and the liquid should be ready to be strained.

Now add 1½ lb. *sugar* to each gallon, and when this has thoroughly dissolved bottle and let it stay uncorked for 14 days, when it should have almost stopped working. Cork and tie down, and in 3 months it will be in excellent condition to drink.

If you wish to improve the colour of the cider, add a slice of *beetroot* to the apples during fermentation.

DANDELION WINE

Pick 3 quarts of *dandelion flower heads* and remove as much of the green calyx as possible. Place the heads in a large bowl and pour over them 1 gallon *water*, which should have been heated to boiling point. The bowl should then be covered with a cloth and left for 3 days, but give the mixture a good stir each day.

On the fourth day add 3 lb. *sugar* and the grated or thinly sliced peel of 2 *lemons* and 1 *orange*. Bring all this to the boil and keep it boiling gently for at least 1 hour, when it should be returned to the bowl and the *juice* of the lemons and the orange added. Use a little of the liquid to dissolve 1 oz. *yeast* and add this to the bowl when the mixture in it is just lukewarm.

Cover again with the cloth and leave in a warm place for 3 days, at the end of which it will be ready to be strained. Before bottling, add 1 lb. *raisins* to the liquid; make sure that an equal quantity of raisins goes into each bottle.

Leave the bottles very lightly corked until fermentation ceases, then make them firm and tie down with wire or string.

This wine should be ready to drink in 6 months, but will be better if kept for a longer period.

ELDERBERRY ROB

Crush out the juice from 6 lb. *ripe elderberries* and to this add 1 lb. *sugar* and mix well. Simmer until the mixture has the consistency of honey. Make a strong drink by adding *boiling water*, 2 parts water to 1 part elderberry rob. If taken before retiring to bed it will induce perspiration and relieve all chest complaints.

ELDERBERRY WINE

Strip the *berries* from the stalks and when you have 7 lb. berries pour over them 2 gallons *water* and leave to stand for 24 hours. Bruise the berries well while they are in the water.

After 24 hours strain through fine muslin, and squeeze the muslin to extract as much of the juice as possible. The liquid should then be put in a pan and to each 2 gallons add 3 lb. *sugar* and 1 *thinly sliced lemon*. Boil 6 *cloves*, ½ oz. *ground ginger*, ½ oz. *whole ginger, bruised*, ½ stick *cinnamon* and 1 lb. *raisins* in a little of the liquid for 20 minutes. Then strain and add to the rest of the wine.

While the liquid is still tepid dissolve 2 tablespoonfuls *yeast* in a little of it and then add to the mixture. Stand the bowl in a warm place, cover with a cloth and leave to ferment for a few days.

When fermentation has ceased, strain or rack off the wine, and bottle. It is wise to cork lightly for a few days to make quite sure all fermentation has ceased, then make the corks firm.

This wine should be ready to drink in 6 months.

HARVESTER'S DRINK

Measure out 1 gallon *water* and place a little of it in a pan with ¼ lb. *oatmeal*, 1 lb. *sugar, juice* and *sliced rind* of 1 *orange* and 1 *lemon* and boil for 10 minutes. Remove from the heat, add the rest of the water and stir well several times until the mixture is cold; then strain and serve.

LAMB'S WOOL (WASSAIL)

Heat 1 quart *ale* and 1 pint *white wine* till hot, then add ½ *nutmeg, grated*, and mix in a small amount of *cinnamon* and *demerara sugar*. Roast some *crab or cider apples* to float on the ale in a deep bowl. Serve very hot.

MEAD

Both mead and metheglin have as their base a simple mixture of *honey* and *water*, made to ferment with a suitable yeast, but there are endless variations in the palatability of the final product, brought about by subtle differences in the manner of preparation, the choice of the type of honey and the use of various herbs and spices at some stage in the making. These include *ginger, mace, cinnamon, cloves, marjoram, balm, caraway seeds* and *hops*. Care should also be taken with the type of water that is used, clean *rain water* being preferable to all others.

The basic method for making mead is as follows: boil the *water* and the *honey* together – 3–6 lb. honey to 1 gallon water, according to the sweetness required – until the honey has completely dissolved. Any flavourings that are required should be added during the boiling process. Then let it cool and add the *yeast* – 1–2 oz. as necessary – creamed with some of the honey water, and place the whole in a clean cask or jar in a warm room to ferment.

When fermentation ceases, remove to somewhere cooler, and leave to stand, covered with a clean cloth, for up to 3 weeks. Then siphon off, making sure the yeast deposit is not disturbed.

Store in a clean cask or jar, and repeat the siphoning process in 6 months' time, when the wine should be bottled, corked down and left for at least another 6 months before drinking.

Generally speaking, a mild flavoured honey is used for making mead, while a stronger flavoured honey is used for making metheglin.

MINT JULEP

Pound *white sugar* and *ice* together – quantities according to sweetness desired – then add 1 wineglass *brandy*, ½ wineglass *rum* and a screw of *lemon rind*. Shake well and serve with sprigs of *bruised mint*.

NETTLE BEER (two kinds)

(a) Take 1 gallon *freshly gathered young nettles*, thoroughly wash them, shake off any excess moisture and dry in a clean cloth. (The nettles in the gallon measure should be fairly firmly packed together.)

Boil the nettles in 1 gallon *water* for not less than 15 minutes. Strain the liquid, pressing the nettles to make sure that all the juice has been extracted, and place in an earthenware fermenting vessel over 1 lb. *demerara sugar* and the *juice* and *grated rind* of 1 *lemon*. Stir well so that all the ingredients are thoroughly mixed, and when lukewarm add 1 oz. *yeast* that has been dissolved in some of the liquid.

Cover the vessel with a thick pad of cloth to exclude the air and keep in a warm place for 3–4 days according to temperature. Strain and bottle, corking firmly.

The beer should be ready to drink after a week.

(b) Gather 2 gallons *young nettles*, thoroughly wash and dry off surplus moisture. Place in a pan with 2 gallons *water*, $\frac{1}{2}$ oz. *root ginger*, 4 lb. *malt*, 2 oz. *hops* and 4 oz. *sarsaparilla*. Bring to the boil and continue to boil for 20 minutes. Strain the mixture and pour over $1\frac{1}{2}$ lb. *sugar* in an earthenware pan. Stir to dissolve sugar. Beat 1 oz. *yeast* into a cream and add to the mixture. Cover and leave in a warm place for 3 days, then bottle and tie corks down.

The beer may be drunk at once, though it improves with keeping.

PARSNIP WINE

Gather 3 lb. *old parsnips* that have been well frosted and scrub them clean. Remove any scabs but do not peel the roots. Cut into thin slices and boil in 1 gallon *water* with 1 oz. *bruised root ginger* and the *rind* (the pith having been removed) from 2 *oranges* and 1 *lemon* until the slices of parsnips are tender.

Strain the liquid on to 3 lb. *demerara sugar*, add the *juice* from the fruit and stir until the sugar is dissolved. When the liquid becomes tepid, dissolve the *yeast* – 1 – 2 oz. as necessary – in a little of the liquid and then add it to the rest.

Place the bowl in a warm place, cover it and leave until fermentation has almost ceased. Then strain or rack off into bottles. Cork lightly until fermentation has quite ceased, then make firm.

This wine is best kept for a year before drinking.

SLOE CORDIAL

Gather the *sloes* on a dry day and place them in jars, covering each layer with *sugar*. When the jar is full, add 1 tablespoonful *brandy* and seal the jar. By the following Christmas the cordial will be ready.

SLOE GIN

Place alternate layers of *pricked sloes* and *fine sugar* until a screw top container is full. When all the sugar has dissolved, add *gin* to cover all the fruit yet leaving a space at the top of the container. Keep in the dark and give the contents a good shake-up at least twice a week for 3 months. Then strain through a flannel, bottle and cork tightly.

The bottles should be stored in a cool dark place for at least a year.

SUGAR BEER

Boil ½ pint *hops* in 1 gallon *water*, then simmer for 2–2½ hours. Sweeten with *honey* and spread a piece of *toast* with 1 oz. *brewer's yeast* and float the toast on the liquid. Cover with a cloth for 24 hours, skim off the froth and the beer is ready to drink.

The beer will only keep for a few days.

WASSAIL BOWL

First bake 2 *apples*. When these are ready heat up 1 quart *ale*, but do not allow it to boil. Then add ¼ oz. *grated nutmeg* and the *grated rind* of 1 *lemon*. Squeeze out the lemon *juice* and add this together with ¼ oz. *ground ginger*, sugar to taste, the 2 baked apples, ½ bottle *sherry* and *toast*. Serve very hot.

A similar wassail bowl can be prepared with *cider* as the base. Half a bottle of *white wine* is preferable to sherry and the lemon can be omitted and replaced with *brandy* to taste.

PART EIGHT

Oddments

CANDLES

You may light another's candle from your own without loss.

Choose neither women nor linen by candlelight.

CHILDBIRTH

If a woman wears her shoes while she is in labour it makes for an easy birth.

COLOURS

Blue is true, Yellow is jealous,
Green's forsaken, Red's brazen,
White is love, And black is death.

Red is a colour that wards off evil spirits and witches. Red ribbons used to be tied to cows' and horses' tails before going out to pasture, and a branch of the rowan tree when the berries were ripe was placed over the cattle pens. Women would tie a thread of red silk round their fingers to keep evil spirits away.

Blue eyes go to skies,
Grey eyes go to Paradise,
Green eyes are doomed to hell,
And black in purgatory dwell.

Green for change and doubleness.

Blue and green should never be seen unless there's a colour in between.

COTTAGES

Great men can come from humble cottages.

ESTATES

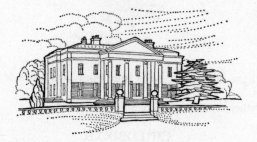

The bones of a great estate are worth picking.

He who walks daily over his estate finds a coin each time.

An estate in two parishes is bread in two wallets.

Land was never lost for the want of an heir.

Many a one for land takes a fool by the hand.

FAMINE

Famine in England begins at the horse manger.

After a famine in the stall, a famine in the hall.

All's good in a famine.

More people die by food than by famine.

Make hunger thy sauce as a medicine for health.

FLOODS

Summer flood never boded England's good.

Make the dam before the flood.

HILLS

Every hill hath its valley.

It is a breezy hill that skirts the down.

The higher the hill the lower the grass.

INNS

He goes not out of his way that goes to a good inn.

A handsome hostess can make a dear reckoning.

ITCHES

An itching nose means that you will soon hear bad news.

An itching foot means that you will soon be going on a journey to a strange place.

LUCK

For good luck, turn your money over when you first hear the cuckoo.

It is unlucky to run past a churchyard.

If a hen should lay a 'cock's' egg a small yolkless egg that can be either the first or the last egg a hen lays) it should be thrown over the roof of the house or ill-luck will be bound to follow.

It is considered very unlucky for a woman to wash her feet while she is pregnant.

It is unlucky to pass a squinting woman unless you speak to her.

It is considered very unlucky if a weasel should cross your path, particularly if it crosses from right to left.

It is unlucky if a black cat crosses your path. However, if it then recrosses your path, the bad luck is dispelled.

It is unlucky to walk under a ladder.

NEVER do the following:

Make a journey on a Friday.

Sit down thirteen to the table at Christmas unless one is pregnant.

Leave a cut onion about the house.

Kill a ladybird.

Leave holly in the house after Candlemas.

Point to the moon.

Carry a spade on your shoulder through the house.

Let a woman help with the curing of bacon while she is pregnant.

Transplant parsley.

MAN

Men are very generous with what costs them nothing.

Men make houses, women make homes.

Men rule the world, women rule men.

When Adam delved and Eve span, who was then the gentleman?

A man of business should not break his word twice.

Though men are made of the same metal they are not cast in the same mould.

No man is always wise, except a fool.

No man can do more than he can.

No man can see above his own height.

No man is born wise or learned.

No man can make a good coat with bad cloth.

No man ever thought his own too much.

No man loveth his fetters, be they made of gold.

Man is the child of error.

Man proposes, God disposes.

He who waits for dead men's shoes will go barefoot a long time.

MARKETS

Buy at a market but sell at home.

A friend at the market is better than money in the chest.

If fools went not to market, bad ware would not be sold.

Two women and a goose make a market.

MARRIAGE

If both partners to a marriage attend church together to hear the banns called, their first child will be an idiot and all the other children will be deaf and dumb.

Those that stick pins where needles ought to go never get married.

Blue vein across his nose, never wears his wedding clothes.

Best in tune when wife is May and husband June.

Choose a good woman's daughter though her father be a devil.

Honest men marry soon, wise men never.

Marry in Lent, live to repent.

Marry above your match and you get a master.

Marry your daughters betimes lest they marry themselves.

Marry your son when you will, your daughter when you can.

It is time to marry when the woman woos the man.

Who marries between sickle and scythe will never thrive.

He who marries for wealth sells liberty.

He who would wed a sot to get a cot will lose cot and keep sot.

Marry a widow before she leaves mourning.

Make haste when you buy a field, but when you marry a wife be slow.

Marry for love and work for silver.

Advise none to marry or to go to war.

When a young man went courting out of his own parish he was expected to pay 'foot ale' to the young men in the parish where his girl lived.

> *When Advent comes do thou refrain,*
> *Till Hilary set thee free again;*
> *Next Septuagesima saith thee nay,*
> *But at Rogation thou must tarry,*
> *Till Trinity shall bid thee marry.*

Marry on:

> *Monday for wealth,*
> *Tuesday for health,*
> *Wednesday the best day of all;*
> *Thursday for losses,*
> *Friday for crosses,*
> *And Saturday no luck at all.*

MILLS and MILLERS

A mill and a wife are always in want of something.

A busy mill does not get grass grown.

Every honest miller has a golden thumb.

Every miller draws water to his own mill.

He is my friend that grinds at my mill.

The miller cannot grind with water that is past.

The mill gains by going, not by standing still.

The miller grinds more than one man's corn.

Much water goeth by the mill that the miller knoweth not of.

POINTS OF THE COMPASS

The North for greatness,
The East for health,
The South for neatness,
The West for wealth.

PORTENTS OF DEATH AND EVIL

If on St Thomas's night [21 December] you cut an apple in two and two of the seeds are damaged, someone in the house will soon be widowed.

All evergreens used for Christmas decorations should be removed by Candlemas Eve. If a leaf or a berry is found after that date a member of the family will surely die.

> *A bloom on the tree when the apples are ripe*
> *Is sure a termination of somebody's life.*

If broom is brought into the house in bloom during the month of May a death will follow.

> *If you sweep in the house with broom in May,*
> *You'll sweep the head of the house away.*

If a hole is found in a cut loaf of bread, it foretells the death of the maker of the bread.

If a girl marries a man with a blue vein across his nose she will almost certainly die before the end of 12 months.

If a rose has leaves among the petals bad luck and even death will attend the family who owns it until the roses bloom again.

If shoes are placed on a table, a death in the house will shortly follow.

If a bird should fly through a room death will follow.

A single snowdrop or primrose brought into the house when they first come into bloom is very unlucky and can herald the death of one of the family.

If white lilac is brought into the house death for one of the inmates will follow.

To bring hawthorn or any other fruit bearing blossoms into the house is a portent of death to one of the inhabitants.

Bees swarming against a wall is a certain sign that there will soon be a death in the house.

When a robin taps on the window, a death will follow.

To do the washing on New Year's day is to court a death in the family.

Ill-luck or even death will fall on the household that has washing about on Good Friday.

When roses and violets flourish in the autumn, it is an evil sign of the coming of plague and pestilence during the coming year.

QUICKNESS

Quick at eating, quick at working.

Some quick wits can digest before others can chew.

Quick and good rarely make good bedfellows.

Quickly come, quickly go.

Take quick steps over miry ground.

More haste less speed.

REPAIRS

He that will not repair a gutter will soon have a house to repair.

He that repairs not a part will have to build all.

RISING

He that hath the name for an early riser may stay in bed till noon.

He that riseth first is first dressed.

The early bird catches the worm.

The early bird catches the late one's breakfast.

He who rises late may need to trot all day.

RIVERS

If you follow the river you come to the sea.

If you cannot see the bottom of a river, do not cross.

Rivers are roads that move.

All rivers need a spring.

A little stream can quench a great thirst.

A stream cannot rise above its spring.

Deep rivers make least noise.

The river past and God forgotten.

Before you drink of a brook it is as well to know its source.

ROADS

No road is long with good company.

The well-used path will be the safest.

Keep to the common road and you are safe.

You cannot be lost on a straight road.

A good road and a wise traveller are two separate things.

Keep to the strait and narrow path.

SELLING

Better sell than be poor.

When folks are ready to buy, you can want to sell.

Who sells the cow must say the word.

When your horse is favoured it is half sold.

He who would sell a blind horse must praise its feet.

SERVANTS

A smiling boy seldom proves to be a good servant.

A servant and a cock should be kept but one year.

An ill servant will never be a good master.

Choose none for servants that have served thy betters.

Grandfather's servants are never good.

A good servant can learn to grow like his master.

He can give little to his servant that licks his knife.

He must serve himself that hath no servant.

He who serves well need not be afraid to ask for his dues.

If you pay not a servant he may pay himself.

> *A servant that is diligent, honest and good,*
> *Sings at his work like a bird on the wood.*

Saturday servants never stay, Sunday servants run away.

SMITHS

It is a poor smith that cannot abide a spark.

The smith has always a spark in his throat.

A smith's mare and a cobbler's wife are always the worst shod.

STICKS

Two dry sticks will kindle a green one.

A straight stick will be crooked in the water.

A stick can help an argument.

There is no argument like that of a stick.

Any stick can beat a dog.

Sticks and stones may break my bones, but words will never hurt me.

STONES

A stone in a well is not lost.

Boil stones in butter and sip the sauce.

No man can stay a stone.

People throw stones at trees with fruit.

238

People in glass houses should not throw stones.

A rolling stone gathers no moss.

A ragged stone grows smooth as it passeth from hand to hand.

Dogs get more angry with stones than with the hands that throw them.

A dull stone can sharpen a dull knife.

When a stone leaves the hand it belongs to the Devil.

A stone that is not in your way need not offend.

TOOLS

It is an ill labourer that quarrels with his tools.

Neither wise nor fools can work without tools.

Only fools will lend their tools.

What is a workman without his tools?

A good reaper deserves a good sickle.

Do not play with edged tools.

There should be no jesting with edged tools or bellropes.

A blunt knife shows a dull wife.

TRADE

A small shop may have a good trade.

A useful trade is like a pot of gold.

Every man to his own trade.

Jack of all trades and master of none.

A man of many trades begs his bread on Sundays.

Good wares find a quick market.

Tailors, millers and weavers are all classed as thieves.

Trade is the mother of money.

Virtue and trade are the best inheritance.

He that hath a trade may travel anywhere.

A trade is better than service.

VALLEYS

He that stays in the valley shall never get over the hill.

Valley sheep are fattest.

VISITORS

If butter is dropped on the floor, it is a sign that you will have a woman visitor. If a knife is dropped you will have a male visitor.

WASHING

Wash all dirty linen at home.

Wash hands often, feet seldom, head never.

You can never wash a blackamoor white.

Dirty water does not wash clean.

The laundress washeth her own smock first.

All dirt can come out in the wash.

Don't wash dirty linen in public.

WATER

All offer water to a drowning dog.

Cast not old water away till new is found.

Foul water will quench a fire.

Hard rocks are worn away by soft water.

He is not thirsty who will not drink water.

In water you may see your face, in wine, the heart of another.

There is no worse water than water that sleeps.

Still waters run deep.

Still water breeds worms.

Smooth runs the water where the water runs deep.

Under water, famine; under snow, bread.

We never know the worth of water till the well runs dry.

He that would have pure water must go to the spring.

Water is a good servant, but a bad master.

A little water sufficeth for moistening clay.

Water afar off quenches not the fire.

Water, fire and soldiers quickly make room.

Shallow waters make most noise.

Never fish in troubled waters.

WELLS

It bodes ill to pump the well dry.

Truth lies at the bottom of the well.

Dig a well before you are thirsty.

When the well is dry, we know the worth of water.

Drawn wells are seldom dry.

The well will run over when it is dry.

WIVES

Choose a wife rather by ear than by eye.

Every man can rule an ill wife but he that has her.

He hath great need of a wife that will marry Mamma's darling.

He that lets his wife go to every feast will not have a good wife.

Husbands are in heaven whose wives chide not.

A mill and a wife are always in want of something.

Choose your wife as you want your children to be.

Sunday wooin' ends in ruin.

WOMEN

A woman and a glass are ever in danger.

A woman and a hen will always be gadding.

A woman, a dog and a walnut tree,
The more you beat them the better they be.

A whistling woman and a crowing hen is good for neither God nor men.

A whistling woman and a crowing hen will drive the Devil out of his den.

A woman's council is not worth much, but the man is mad that doth not take it.

A woman's mind and a winter's wind changeth often.

Women and girls must be praised whether it is true or not.

Women and bairns keep counsel of what they know not.

Women laugh when they can and weep when they will.

Women, like the moon, shine on borrowed light.

Women, priests and poultry are never satisfied.

Choose neither women nor linen by candlelight.

One tongue is enough for a woman.

Discreet women have neither eyes nor ears.

Women and wine drive men out of their wits.

There is many a light heart under a black veil.

WOOD

You cannot see the wood for the trees.

If you chop your own wood it will warm you twice.

Wood half burned is soonest kindled.

He that would live longest should fetch his wood furthest.

Little wood, much fruit.

Do not halloo till you are out of the wood.

TERMS FOR THE LAND

These terms often form part of place-names, thereby describing the type of country in which the places are located.

Barrow: An ancient or prehistoric burial mound; a tumulus; a hill (now chiefly in place-names).

Beck: A brook.

Berry: Mound, hillock or barrow.

Borough (in Scotland *burgh*): A fortress, castle or citadel; a fortified town.

Brake: A clump of bushes, brushwood, or briers; a thicket.

Broad: In East Anglia, a piece of fresh water formed by the broadening out of a river.

Bush: A thicket; land overgrown with bushes.

Car: Marshy land that is overgrown with bushes etc.

Close: An enclosure about or beside a building.

Coppice: A wood, thicket or plantation of small trees or bushes.

Copse: As coppice.

Croft: A small piece of enclosed land for tillage or pasture etc., usually attached to a house.

Dale: A hollow or valley; a portion of land, specifically an undivided field indicated by landmarks only.

Dell: A small valley, a vale, especially a wooded one.

Dene: A bare sandy tract or low sandhill near the sea.

Dyke (*dike*): An embankment for restraining sea or river water, a ditch.

Dumble: A hollow; a shady dell; a wooded valley.

End: The outlying part of an estate or farm.

Erg: A hill pasture; land used only for summer grazing.

Farrow: A path.

Fit: Grassland beside a river.

Fold: A pen or enclosure for domestic animals.

Garston: A grass enclosure; a paddock.

Gore: A triangular piece of land.

Green: A plot of grassy ground.

Ground: A piece or parcel of land; enclosed land surrounding or attached to a building, serving chiefly for ornament or recreation.

Ham: A riverside meadow.

Hanger: A wood on the side of a steep hill or bank.

Hatch: A wicket gate or a piece of land that is gained by a wicket gate.

Haugh: A piece of flat alluvial land by the side of a river, forming part of the floor of the river valley.

Haw: A hedge; a piece of land enclosed by a hedge.

Hay: A hedge or fence; a fenced piece of land, a park, an enclosure.

Hern (hyrne): A nook or corner of land.

Hide (hyde): A measure of land in Old English times – an area sufficient to support one free family and its dependants, defined as being as much land as could be tilled with one plough in a year. The hide was normally 100 acres, but the size of the acre itself varied.

Holm (holme): A meadow on the seashore.

Holt: A wood, a thicket.

Hoo (hough): The end of a ridge where the land begins to fall sharply.

Hop: A piece of enclosed marshland.

Hurst (hirst): A hillock, knoll or bank, especially a sandy one; a ford made by a bed of sand or shingle; a grove of trees, a copse, wood or wooded eminence.

Ing: A meadow, especially one beside a river and low-lying: meadow-land.

Jack: Unused land.

Knap: The summit of a hill; a hillock or knoll, rising ground.

Knoll: The rounded top of a mountain or hill; a small rounded eminence.

Lagger: Resting place.

Lea: A tract of open ground, whether meadow, pasture or arable land; land that has remained untilled for some time, arable land under grass.

Leasow: Pasture or meadow-land.

Main: Land held in demesne.

Mead: Land kept permanently covered with grass which is mown for use as hay, i.e. meadow-land.

Nook: A corner of land; a small triangular field; a headland or promontory; a piece of land projecting from one division into another and terminating in a point.

Over: A slope, hill or ridge; a river bank.

Pasture: A piece of grassland reserved for cattle and sheep to graze on.

Piece: An allotment or portion of land, enclosed, marked off by bounds, or viewed as distinct.

Pike: A mountain or hill with a pointed summit.

Pilch: A triangular field.

Plantation: An area of growing plants of any kind which have been planted, now used especially to refer to a wood of planted trees.

Plash: A marshy pool; waterlogged land.

Pleck: A small piece of land.

Reading: Waste land taken into cultivation.

Rean: Land on a boundary.

Ridge: A raised or rounded strip of arable land, usually one of a series, with intermediate open furrows, into which a field is divided by ploughing in a special manner.

Rood: About a quarter of an acre of land, the exact amount varies locally.

Royd: A clearing in woodland.

Screed: A strip of land; a parcel of ground.

Shaw (shay): A thicket, small wood, copse or grove.

Shot: A block of arable land.

Sling: A loop or curving piece of land.

Slough: A boggy piece of land.

Tye: An enclosure or pasture.

Wick: A farm, specifically a dairy farm; a town, village or hamlet.

Yard: An enclosure forming a pen for cattle or poultry, a place for storing hay etc., attached to a farmhouse, or surrounded by farm buildings.

Yield: Sloping ground.

Index

50 11